WYDANIE NARODOWE
DZIEŁ FRYDERYKA CHOPINA

NATIONAL EDITION
OF THE WORKS OF FRYDERYK CHOPIN

POLONAISE in E♭ Op. 22
preceded with ANDANTE SPIANATO
FOR PIANO AND ORCHESTRA
version for one piano

NATIONAL EDITION
Edited by JAN EKIER

Foundation
for the National Edition
of the Works of Fryderyk Chopin

PWM
EDITION

SERIES A. WORKS PUBLISHED DURING CHOPIN'S LIFETIME. VOLUME XIVb

FRYDERYK CHOPIN

POLONEZ Es-dur Op. 22
poprzedzony ANDANTE SPIANATO
NA FORTEPIAN I ORKIESTRĘ
wersja na jeden fortepian

WYDANIE NARODOWE
Redaktor naczelny: JAN EKIER

FUNDACJA WYDANIA NARODOWEGO
POLSKIE WYDAWNICTWO MUZYCZNE SA
WARSZAWA 2023

SERIA A. UTWORY WYDANE ZA ŻYCIA CHOPINA. TOM XIVb

Redakcja tomu: Jan Ekier, Paweł Kamiński

Komentarz wykonawczy i Komentarz źródłowy (skrócony) dołączone są do nut głównej
serii *Wydania Narodowego* oraz do strony internetowej www.chopin-nationaledition.com

Pełne *Komentarze źródłowe* do poszczególnych tomów wydawane są oddzielnie.

Wydany w oddzielnym tomie *Wstęp do Wydania Narodowego Dzieł Fryderyka Chopina
– 1. Zagadnienia edytorskie* obejmuje całokształt ogólnych problemów wydawniczych,
zaś *Wstęp… – 2. Zagadnienia wykonawcze* – całokształt ogólnych problemów interpretacyjnych.
Pierwsza część *Wstępu* jest także dostępna na stronie www.pwm.com.pl

Partytura *Poloneza* tworzy tom 22 **A XVf**, a wersja z wyciągiem fortepianowym
znajduje sie w tomie *Utwory Koncertowe* 32 **B VII**.

Editors of this Volume: Jan Ekier, Paweł Kamiński

A *Performance Commentary* and a *Source Commentary (abridged)* are included in the
music of the main series of the *National Edition* and available on www.chopin-nationaledition.com

Full *Source Commentaries* on each volume are published separately.

The *Introduction to the National Edition of the Works of Fryderyk Chopin,
1. Editorial Problems*, published as a separate volume, covers general matters concerning the publication.
The *Introduction… 2. Problems of Performance* covers all general questions of the interpretation.
First part of the *Introduction* is also available on the website www.pwm.com.pl

The score of the *Polonaise* forms the volume 22 **A XVf**, and the version with the piano arrangement
is to be found in the *Concert Works* 32 **B VII**.

Polonez Es-dur op. 22 / Polonaise in E♭ major Op. 22

ANDANTE SPIANATO

page / s. 10

POLONAISE

page / s. 16

about the Polonaise ...

Op. 22

"I started writing a Polonaise for piano and orchestra, but it only gins; there is a ginning but no beginning."

From F. Chopin's letter to Tytus Woyciechowski in Poturzyn, Warsaw, 18 September 1830.

o Polonezie ...

op. 22

„Zacząłem Poloneza z orkiestrą, ale tylko dopiero się cznie, jest cząstek, ale początku nie ma."

Z listu F. Chopina do Tytusa Woyciechowskiego w Poturzynie, Warszawa 18 IX 1830.

Grande polonaise brillante

précédée d'un Andante spianato,

pour le Piano avec accompagnement d'Orchestre

A Madame d'Est

ANDANTE SPIANATO

Tranquillo ♩.= 69 (*ossia:* 63)

op. 22

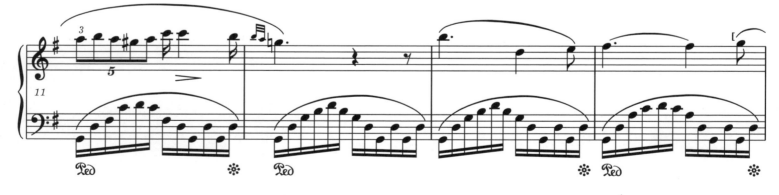

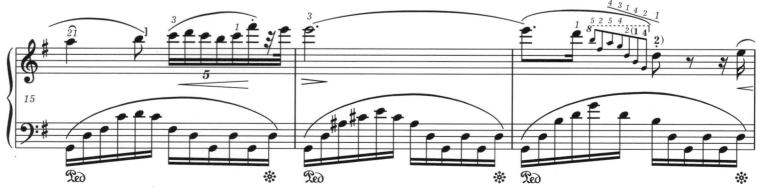

Semplice

[POLONAISE]

FWN 16 **A XIVb**

* Inne palcowanie – patrz *Komentarz wykonawczy*.
  For a different fingering *vide Performance Commentary*.

18

* Wersja oryginalna: (skala fortepianu Chopina sięgała w tym czasie tylko do *f⁴*).
The original version: (at that time the compass of Chopin's piano reached only to *f⁴*).

FWN 16 **A XIVb**

* Inne odczytanie rytmu:
  A different reading of the rhythm:

poco ritenuto e dim.

NATIONAL EDITION OF THE WORKS OF FRYDERYK CHOPIN

Plan of the edition

Series A. WORKS PUBLISHED DURING CHOPIN'S LIFETIME

Series B. WORKS PUBLISHED POSTHUMOUSLY

(The titles in square brackets [] have been reconstructed by the National Edition; the titles in slant marks // are still in use today but are definitely, or very probably, not authentic)

1 **A I**   **Ballades** Opp. 23, 38, 47, 52

2 **A II**   **Etudes** Opp. 10, 25, Three Etudes (Méthode des Méthodes)

3 **A III**   **Impromptus** Opp. 29, 36, 51

4 **A IV**   **Mazurkas (A)** Opp. 6, 7, 17, 24, 30, 33, 41, Mazurka in a (Gaillard), Mazurka in a (from the album La France Musicale /Notre Temps/), Opp. 50, 56, 59, 63

25 **B I**   **Mazurkas (B)** in B♭, G, a, C, F, G, B♭, A♭, C, a, g, f

5 **A V**   **Nocturnes** Opp. 9, 15, 27, 32, 37, 48, 55, 62

6 **A VI**   **Polonaises (A)** Opp. 26, 40, 44, 53, 61

26 **B II**   **Polonaises (B)** in B♭, g, A♭, g♯, d, f, b♭, B♭, G♭

7 **A VII**   **Preludes** Opp. 28, 45

8 **A VIII**   **Rondos** Opp. 1, 5, 16

9 **A IX**   **Scherzos** Opp. 20, 31, 39, 54

10 **A X**   **Sonatas** Opp. 35, 58

11 **A XI**   **Waltzes (A)** Opp. 18, 34, 42, 64

27 **B III**   **Waltzes (B)** in E, b, D♭, A♭, e, G♭, A♭, f, a

12 **A XII**   **Various Works (A)** Variations brillantes Op. 12, Bolero, Tarantella, Allegro de concert, Fantaisie Op. 49, Berceuse, Barcarolle; *supplement* – Variation VI from "Hexameron"

28 **B IV**   **Various Works (B)** Variations in E, Sonata in c (Op. 4)

29 **B V**   **Various Compositions** Funeral March in c, [Variants] /Souvenir de Paganini/, Nocturne in e, Ecossaises in D, G, D♭, Contredanse, [Allegretto], Lento con gran espressione /Nocturne in c♯/, Cantabile in B♭, Presto con leggierezza /Prelude in A♭/, Impromptu in c♯ /Fantaisie-Impromptu/, "Spring" (version for piano), Sostenuto /Waltz in E♭/, Moderato /Feuille d'Album/, Galop Marquis, Nocturne in c

13 **A XIIIa** **Concerto in E minor** Op. 11 for piano and orchestra (version for one piano)

30 **B VIa**   **Concerto in E minor** Op. 11 for piano and orchestra (version with second piano)

14 **A XIIIb** **Concerto in F minor** Op. 21 for piano and orchestra (version for one piano)

31 **B VIb**   **Concerto in F minor** Op. 21 for piano and orchestra (version with second piano)

15 **A XIVa** **Concert Works** for piano and orchestra Opp. 2, 13, 14 (version for one piano)

32 **B VII**   **Concert Works** for piano and orchestra Opp. 2, 13, 14, 22 (version with second piano)

16 **A XIVb** **Grande Polonaise in E♭ major** Op. 22 for piano and orchestra (version for one piano)

17 **A XVa**   **Variations on "Là ci darem" from "Don Giovanni"** Op. 2. Score

18 **A XVb**   **Concerto in E minor** Op. 11. Score (historical version)

33 **B VIIIa** **Concerto in E minor** Op. 11. Score (concert version)

19 **A XVc**   **Fantasia on Polish Airs** Op. 13. Score

20 **A XVd**   **Krakowiak** Op. 14. Score

21 **A XVe**   **Concerto in F minor** Op. 21. Score (historical version)

34 **B VIIIb** **Concerto in F minor** Op. 21. Score (concert version)

22 **A XVf**   **Grande Polonaise in E♭ major** Op. 22. Score

23 **A XVI**   **Works for Piano and Cello** Polonaise Op. 3, Grand Duo Concertant, Sonata Op. 65

35 **B IX**   **Rondo in C** for two pianos; **Variations in D** for four hands; *addendum* – working version of Rondo in C (for one piano)

24 **A XVII** **Piano Trio** Op. 8

36 **B X**   **Songs**

37 **Supplement** Compositions partly by Chopin: Hexameron, Mazurkas in F♯, D, D, C, Variations for Flute and Piano; harmonizations of songs and dances: "The Dąbrowski Mazurka", "God who hast embraced Poland" (Largo) Bourrées in G, A, Allegretto in A-major/minor

Bar 31 R.H. **FE** (→**EE**1,**GE**) mistakenly has bb^2-d^3 instead of bb^2-eb^3 as the demisemiquaver before the fourth quaver of the bar.
R.H. The first editions still have the accent below a^1 on the sixth quaver of the bar. The absence of a corresponding accent in analogous bar 175 indicates the possible engraver's error in the bar discussed, since in **[A]** the reprise of the *Polonaise* (bars 162-220) was presumably not written in notes. Cf. bars 69-70 and analog., in which the accenting of notes on the sixth quaver of the bar is linked with a prolongation of their rhythmic value.

Bars 32 and 176 In bar 32 the L.H.'s bb is not tied in the sources; besides, **GE**2 (→**GE**3) missed the tie next to bb^1 in the R.H. Some of the later collected editions also omitted corresponding ties in analogous bar 176.

p. 18 *Bars 42 and 186* R.H. The sources have the figures 2 and 4 above the d^2-f^2 third. This fingering, not connected naturally either with the previous trill nor with the following figure, is evidently mistaken; presumably, it should be situated above the next c^2-eb^2 third.

p. 19 *Bar 56 and 200* R.H. In **EE** there is no grace-note before eb^3 and the sign of the turn is given between eb^2 and eb^3. In **GE** this version is found only in bar 200. We cannot exclude the possibility that this is the original version, changed by Chopin in the last correction of **FE** (cf. the last part of the next comment).

Bar 57 and 201 R.H. In the first editions the note bb^2 on the second quaver of the bar has the value of a crotchet. Nonetheless, in **FE** (→**GE**) the figuration, written in small notes and filling the second part of the bar, is laid out in such a way as if the sustained bb^2 beginning it was to coincide already with the third quaver of the bar (in **EE** the arrangement of the passage is essentially identical, and lacks only this opening bb^2). Upon this basis, one of the later collected editions arbitrarily reduced the value of bb^2 on the second quaver of the bar to a quaver. The following arguments speak against such a solution:
– a rhythmic scheme, characteristic of the main theme of the *Polonaise*, in which the revival of melodic motion, halted on the first or second quaver of the bar, does not take place until the fourth quaver; such a scheme occurs in bars 17-18, 21-22, 25 and 27 and primarily in bar 19, analogous to the discussed bar;
– errors in planning the L.H. in relation to the R.H. were made in **FE**, slight imprecision is to be found in *Andante spianato* (bar 15), and a more serious mistake is encountered in, e. g *Nocturne in Bb minor*, Op. 9 no. 1, bar 73.
R.H. The third and second penultimate notes of the passage in **EE** are ab^2 and g^2. **GE** has this version only in bar 201. This is probably the original version, changed by Chopin in the last proof-reading of **FE**.

Bar 62 and 206 R.H. The last small note in **EE** is a^2.

p. 20 *Bar 84* R.H. Unquestionably, only the limited range of the piano compelled Chopin to resign from transferring the chord an octave higher, an operation natural from the viewpoint of execution and characteristic of virtuoso cadences.

p. 21 *Bar 90* R.H. Some of the later collected editions arbitrarily changed the last quaver from b^2 to b^3.

Bar 92 R.H. In **FE** (→**EE**,**GE**1) there is no ♮ prior to the eighth note from the end of the bar. This is certainly Chopin's omission, since starting from the sixth small note the figuration has an established G-major key with distinctly shown e^2 sounds (the seventh and thirteenth small notes).

Bar 93 and 94 In **FE** the absence of the ties sustaining d in bar 93 and b in bar 94 seems to be accidental. **EE** and **GE**2 (→**GE**3) supplemented the tie in bar 93, and in bar 94 **GE** added a tie next to b but omitted it next to G.

Bar 95 The mistaken rhythmic record in **FE**:

can be read in two ways:
– with a quaver at the beginning of the bar (according to the L.H.), recognising the three semiquavers following it as a triplet; in the main text we give this version, contained in **EE** and **GE**, due to its association with a polonaise rhythm and a rhythmic analogy to the previous two bars;
– with a semiquaver at the beginning of the bar (according to the R.H.), which seems to be indicated by the distances between the notes in **FE**.

p. 22 *Bar 101* R.H. **EE**2 and the majority of the later collected editions arbitrarily changed the last note of the bar from g^3 to f^3. The original version most probably does not contain a mistake – cf. similar devices in passages of this type in *Etude in C*, Op. 10 no. 1, bar 5 and 29.

p. 24 *Bar 128* L.H. **FE** (→**EE**) has f at the beginning of the bar. Chopin corrected this error in **FE**D. **GE** also contains the proper version.

Bar 132 L.H. In **GE**1 there is no ledger line below the minim eb^1 so that **GE**2 (→**GE**3) mistakenly deciphered and printed it as c^1.

p. 25 *Bar 142* R.H. The mordent above g^1 is found only in **FE**.
R.H. There are no accidentals prior to the fourth and eight quaver in **FE** (→**EE**,**GE**). Some of the later collected editions arbitrarily added naturals before those notes thus establishing their sound as c^2 and c^3. We are entitled to presume that in the entire passage Chopin regarded ♯, raising c^3 to $c\#^3$ at the beginning of the bar, as binding; this is proven by the following arguments:
– ♮ placed before c^4, the last note of the bar, shows that not until this spot did Chopin consider it necessary to restore c;
– in the sources for the *Polonaise*, where an octave transposition sign is used, the accidentals remain binding at a pitch following from the record, which in this case signifies the reading of the fourth semiquaver as $c\#^2$; since an exact repetition of the figure an octave higher does not give rise to even the slightest doubts, the eighth semiquaver should be $c\#^3$, and leaving it without a sign is only a slight imprecision in the notation;
– we come across a similar situation in the autographs of *Concerto in F minor*, Op. 21, first movement, bars 143-144, where in a figure transferred by an octave Chopin omitted the indispensable ♯, raising f^2 to $f\#^2$, and in the next bar cancelled the still heard sharps in the proofs of one of the editions.
Taking the above mentioned arguments into consideration we give the version with $c\#$ indubitably intended by Chopin, supplementing it with sharps in accordance with the contemporary principles of chromatic spelling.

p. 27 *Bar 161* R.H. **EE** does not have one of the g^1 grace-notes.

Jan Ekier
Paweł Kamiński

4

SOURCE COMMENTARY /ABRIDGED/

Introductory comments

The following commentary sets out in an abridged form the principles of editing the musical text and discusses the most important discrepancies between the authentic sources; furthermore, it draws attention to departures from the authentic text which are most frequently encountered in the collected editions of Chopin's music compiled after his death. A separately published *Source Commentary* contains a detailed description of the sources, their filiation, justification of the choice of primary sources, a thorough presentation of the differences between them and a reproduction of characteristic fragments.

Abbreviations: R.H. – right hand, L.H. – left hand. The sign → symbolises a connection between sources; it should be read "and ... based on it".

Polonaise in E flat major, Op. 22

Sources
[A] There is no extant autograph.
FE First French edition, M. Schlesinger (M. S. 1926), Paris July 1836. **FE** is based on **[A]** and was corrected by Chopin probably twice.
FED Copy from the collection belonging to Chopin's pupil Camille Dubois (Bibliothèque Nationale, Paris). It contains fingering originating from lessons given by Chopin, a corrected printing error, and minor performance directives.
EE1 First English edition, Wessel & C° (W & C° N° 1643), London August 1836, based most probably on the proofs of **FE** without Chopin's final corrections. It includes a number of adjustments; Chopin did not participate in its production.
EE2 Second impression of **EE**1 (same firm and number), ca. 1856-60, with few changes.
EE = **EE**1 and **EE**2.
GE1 First German edition, Breitkopf & Härtel (5709), Leipzig August 1836. Based on **FE** it contains traces of the publisher's adjustments and a number of errors. Chopin took no part in its production. There are copies of **GE**1 with different details on the covers (three versions).
GE2 Second German edition, (same firm and number), ca. 1860-65, containing the text of **GE**1 with slight adjustments and several errors.
GE3 Later impression of **GE**2, ca. 1866. It corrects some of the errors, supplements accidentals, and introduces certain arbitrary changes.
GE = **GE**1, **GE**2 and **GE**3.
Sco Manuscript of the score of the *Polonaise* (Österreichische Nationalbibliothek, Vienna), prepared as a base for its first edition (Breitkopf & Härtel, 1880) most probably in the 1870s. The solo part was copied from **GE**3 and subjected to further adjustments.

Editorial Principles
We accept as our basis **FE** as the only authentic source, and take into consideration Chopin's annotations in **FE**D.
A precise distinction of the long and short accents, characteristic for Chopin, as well as their assignment to the right or left hand is impossible due to the absence of an autograph and the visible imprecision of the first editions. We attempt to recreate the intention of the composer by taking in consideration his habits, documented in sources for other compositions.

Andante spianato

p. 10
Bar 1 The value of the metronomic tempo given in parentheses, lower than the one printed in **FE** (→**EE,GE**), was added by Chopin into **FE**D.

p. 11
Bar 27 L.H. Two versions of Chopin's fingering correspond to two possible readings of figures imprecisely written into **FE**D.

p. 12
Bars 36-37 The pedalling in **FE** (→**GE**1) is recorded imprecisely – after the sign ℞ at the end of bar 36 there occurs a successive such sign at the beginning of bar 37. Possibly, the sign ✳ at the end of bar 36 is missing although it is quite probable that it was the sign ℞ in bar 37 which was unnecessarily put by the engraver of **FE**. Chopin used similar pedalling upon numerous occasions, e. g. in *Nocturne in F*, Op. 15 no. 1, bars 72-73, *Ballade in F minor*, Op. 52, bars 12-13, *Sonata in B minor*, Op. 58, third movement, bars 118-119. The version without the pedal change in bar 37 is found in **EE**.

Bar 43 R.H. It is doubtful whether the value of the first a^2 (♩·), occurring in the sources, is not mistaken. In the whole *Andante* the passages written with small notes fill the given rhythmic value, thus designating both the moment of their beginning and ending. Here, the rhythmic values and hence the moment of beginning the ornament are not defined. Taking into consideration arguments provided by sources – the probable reasons for the errors committed by the engraver, and musical arguments – the tempo of the performance comparable with the tempo of figures in bar 17 or 41, it seems most fitting of all to recognise the two notations in the *Performance Commentary*.

p. 13
Bars 55-56, 59-60 and analog. R.H. Certain later collected editions arbitrarily distinguished the fourth and tenth semiquavers in those bars by means of additional stems. Cf. *Performance Commentary*.

Bars 56 and 100 R.H. The tenth note in **GE**3 was changed arbitrarily from $f\#^1$ to a^1.

p. 14
Bar 78 and 90 In the notation in **FE** (→**EE,GE**):

those bars could be mistakenly played in 4/4 time. We render this notation more precise in order to avoid ambiguity.

Polonaise

p. 16
Bars 1-16 In the sources the version intended for a single piano does not contain any markings as regards instrumentation in those fragments, which in the concert version are performed without the solo piano. We add the markings upon the basis of original orchestral parts in those cases where indicating the intended authentic instrumentation could prove to be inspiring for the pianist (bars 1 and 15).

Bar 20, 58 and analog. L.H. In the sources the prolongation of the crotchet *f* to the fifth quaver of the bar is noted imprecisely. In **FE** (→**GE**) this note is prolonged only in bar 20 (by means of a dot) and 164 (by means of a tie and a note). As a result of errors and omissions there are no prolongations in **EE**. Performance differentiation was certainly not Chopin's intention and thus we render the script of this detail uniform by following the example of bar 164.

p. 17
Bar 29 R.H. We change the *tr* sign, which occurs in the first editions probably due to a mistake, into ᴧᴧ, found in all the analogous bars in the sources. A differentiation of such signs in Chopin's autographs can pose a difficult task (cf. for instance *Waltzes in A minor*, Op. 34 no. 2, bars 37, 39 and analog., and in D♭, Op. 64 no. 1, bar 20 and 92), and has sometimes caused problems for the engravers of the first editions (e. g. in *Waltz in A♭*, Op. 34 no. 1, bar 40 and analog.).

3

PERFORMANCE COMMENTARY

Notes on the musical text

The v a r i a n t s marked as *ossia* were given this label by Chopin or were added in his hand to pupils' copies; variants without this designation are the result of discrepancies in the texts of authentic versions or an inability to establish an unambiguous reading of the text.

Minor authentic alternatives (single notes, ornaments, slurs, accents, pedal indications, etc.) that can be regarded as variants are enclosed in round brackets (), whilst editorial additions are written in square brackets []. Pianists who are not interested in editorial questions, and want to base their performance on a single text, unhampered by variants, are recommended to use the music printed in the principal staves, including all the markings in brackets.

Chopin's original f i n g e r i n g is indicated in large bold-type numerals, **1 2 3 4 5,** in contrast to the editors' fingering which is written in small italic numerals *1 2 3 4 5*. Wherever authentic fingering is enclosed in parentheses this means that it was not present in the primary sources, but added by Chopin to his pupils' copies. The dashed signs indicating the distribution of parts between the hands come from the editors.

A general discussion on the interpretation of Chopin's works is to be contained in a separate volume: *The Introduction to the National Edition*, in the section entitled *Problems of Performance*.

Abbreviations: R.H. – right hand, L.H. – left hand.

Andante spianato

In all his works only once did Chopin use the term *spianato* ("smoothed, even"). In this case, its purpose was probably to bring the performance closer to the unique ambience of the composition, created by, i. a. dynamics, tone colour, pedalling and phrasing. Particular attention should be paid to the subtle realisation of the authentic slurring. As a rule, short slurs, characteristic for this period in Chopin's oeuvre, do not embrace the whole phrases – hence although the beginning of the slurs should be slightly emphasised, the performers must be warned against releasing the hand when the end of a slur occurs within a phrase.

p. 10   *Bar 12 and 44* R.H. The grace-note *b²* should be sounded together with *G* in the L.H.

p. 11   *Bar 19, 20, 30 and 32* R.H. The grace-notes should be executed lightly in order not to disturb the rhythm (bar 19) or obliterate the impression of an accent on the subsequent note. It is less essential whether striking them will coincide with an appropriate note in the L.H. or slightly earlier.

Bars 20-21 L.H. The editors recommend to apply a "harmonic legato" at the end of bar 20 (the fingers sustain the components of harmony) so as to accentuate the modulating transition of the bass: 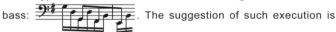. The suggestion of such execution is contained in the *sempre legato* marking, written in bar 1 and binding throughout this whole section.

p. 12   *Bar 43* R.H. The rhythmic solution of the first half of the bar:

Cf. *Source Commentary.*

Bar 48 R.H. The grace-note *c#²* should be struck together with *G* in the L.H.

p. 13   *Bars 55-56, 59-62 and analog.* R.H. The accented *d²* notes should create an independent sonoric plan. Chopin applied a similar device upon several occasions – cf., e. g. *Polonaise in A♭*, Op. 53, bars 143-151 or *Berceuse in D♭*, Op. 57, bars 53-54. The additional distinction of the lowest notes of the figuration, proposed by some editors, obliterates the effect intended by Chopin, concurrent with the titular *spianato*.

p. 15   *Last bar* Arpeggios should be executed continuously from *G₁* to *g¹*.

Polonaise

p. 17   *Bar 26 and analog.* In order not to blur the difference between those bars and bar 28 and analog. the grace-notes should be executed in an anticipatory manner.

p. 18   *Bar 41* R.H. Beginning of trill: *d²-f²* together with *a-e♭¹* in the L.H.

Bars 51-54 In bar 54 the accented notes *f²* and *f#²* can be executed with the L.H.

Different fingering of bars 51-53:

and bars 53-54:

p. 19   *Bar 61* R.H. It seems more likely that Chopin envisaged the following performance:

The following execution, however, may be permitted:

Bars 61-62 In the opinion of the editors the passage is best arranged in such a way that *g²* would coincide with *E♭* at the beginning of bar 62, and *g³* with *b♭-g¹* on the third quaver of this bar.

p. 23   *Bars 125-126* R.H. It is better to execute the grace-notes in an anticipatory manner.

p. 24   *Bar 131* R.H. Beginning of trill: *b¹* together with the octave in the L.H.

p. 27   *Bar 161* R.H. The first *g¹* grace-note should be struck simultaneously with *E♭* in the L.H., as it was marked by Chopin in a pupil's copy in similar bar 55.

p. 35   *Bars 269-272* In the opinion of the editors the semiquavers in the L.H. can be performed simultaneously with the last semiquavers in each group in the R.H. Cf. a similar figuration at the end of *Variations in B♭*, Op. 12.

Jan Ekier, Paweł Kamiński

FRYDERYK CHOPIN
POLONAISE in E♭ Op. 22

Performance Commentary
Source Commentary (abridged)

WYDANIE NARODOWE DZIEŁ FRYDERYKA CHOPINA

Plan edycji

Seria A. UTWORY WYDANE ZA ŻYCIA CHOPINA

Seria B. UTWORY WYDANE POŚMIERTNIE

(Tytuły w nawiasach kwadratowych [] są tytułami zrekonstruowanymi przez WN, tytuły w nawiasach prostych // są dotychczas używanymi, z pewnością lub dużym prawdopodobieństwem, nieautentycznymi tytułami)

1 **A I**	**Ballady** op. 23, 38, 47, 52	
2 **A II**	**Etiudy** op. 10, 25, Trzy Etiudy (Méthode des Méthodes)	
3 **A III**	**Impromptus** op. 29, 36, 51	
4 **A IV**	**Mazurki (A)** op. 6, 7, 17, 24, 30, 33, 41, Mazurek a (Gaillard), Mazurek a (z albumu La France Musicale /Notre Temps/), op. 50, 56, 59, 63	25 **B I** **Mazurki (B)** B, G, a, C, F, G, B, As, C, a, g, f
5 **A V**	**Nokturny** op. 9, 15, 27, 32, 37, 48, 55, 62	
6 **A VI**	**Polonezy (A)** op. 26, 40, 44, 53, 61	26 **B II** **Polonezy (B)** B, g, As, gis, d, f, b, B, Ges
7 **A VII**	**Preludia** op. 28, 45	
8 **A VIII**	**Ronda** op. 1, 5, 16	
9 **A IX**	**Scherza** op. 20, 31, 39, 54	
10 **A X**	**Sonaty** op. 35, 58	
11 **A XI**	**Walce (A)** op. 18, 34, 42, 64	27 **B III** **Walce (B)** E, h, Des, As, e, Ges, As, f, a
12 **A XII**	**Dzieła różne (A)** Variations brillantes op. 12, Bolero, Tarantela, Allegro de concert, Fantazja op. 49, Berceuse, Barkarola; *suplement* – Wariacja VI z „Hexameronu"	28 **B IV** **Dzieła różne (B)** Wariacje E, Sonata c (op. 4)
		29 **B V** **Różne utwory** Marsz żałobny c, [Warianty] /Souvenir de Paganini/, Nokturn e, Ecossaises D, G, Des, Kontredans, [Allegretto], Lento con gran espressione /Nokturn cis/, Cantabile B, Presto con leggierezza /Preludium As/, Impromptu cis /Fantaisie-Impromptu/, „Wiosna" (wersja na fortepian), Sostenuto /Walc Es/, Moderato /Kartka z albumu/, Galop Marquis, Nokturn c
13 **A XIIIa**	**Koncert e-moll** op. 11 na fortepian i orkiestrę (wersja na jeden fortepian)	30 **B VIa** **Koncert e-moll** op. 11 na fortepian i orkiestrę (wersja z drugim fortepianem)
14 **A XIIIb**	**Koncert f-moll** op. 21 na fortepian i orkiestrę (wersja na jeden fortepian)	31 **B VIb** **Koncert f-moll** op. 21 na fortepian i orkiestrę (wersja z drugim fortepianem)
15 **A XIVa**	**Utwory koncertowe** na fortepian i orkiestrę op. 2, 13, 14 (wersja na jeden fortepian)	32 **B VII** **Utwory koncertowe** na fortepian i orkiestrę op. 2, 13, 14, 22 (wersja z drugim fortepianem)
16 **A XIVb**	**Polonez Es-dur** op. 22 na fortepian i orkiestrę (wersja na jeden fortepian)	
17 **A XVa**	**Wariacje na temat z** *Don Giovanniego* **Mozarta** op. 2. Partytura	
18 **A XVb**	**Koncert e-moll** op. 11. Partytura (wersja historyczna)	33 **B VIIIa** **Koncert e-moll** op. 11. Partytura (wersja koncertowa)
19 **A XVc**	**Fantazja na tematy polskie** op. 13. Partytura	
20 **A XVd**	**Krakowiak** op. 14. Partytura	
21 **A XVe**	**Koncert f-moll** op. 21. Partytura (wersja historyczna)	34 **B VIIIb** **Koncert f-moll** op. 21. Partytura (wersja koncertowa)
22 **A XVf**	**Polonez Es-dur** op. 22. Partytura	
23 **A XVI**	**Utwory na fortepian i wiolonczelę** Polonez op. 3, Grand Duo Concertant, Sonata op. 65	35 **B IX** **Rondo C-dur** na dwa fortepiany; **Wariacje D-dur** na 4 ręce; *dodatek* – wersja robocza Ronda C-dur (na jeden fortepian)
24 **A XVII**	**Trio na fortepian, skrzypce i wiolonczelę** op. 8	36 **B X** **Pieśni i piosnki**

37 **Suplement** Utwory częściowego autorstwa Chopina: Hexameron, Mazurki Fis, D, D, C, Wariacje na flet i fortepian; harmonizacje pieśni i tańców: „Mazurek Dąbrowskiego", „Boże, coś Polskę" (Largo), Bourrées G, A, Allegretto A-dur/a-moll

Okładka i opracowanie graficzne · Cover design and graphics: MARIA EKIER
Tłumaczenie angielskie · English translation: ALEKSANDRA RODZIŃSKA-CHOJNOWSKA

Fundacja Wydania Narodowego Dzieł Fryderyka Chopina
ul. Okólnik 2, pok. 405, 00-368 Warszawa
www.chopin-nationaledition.com

Polskie Wydawnictwo Muzyczne SA
al. Krasińskiego 11a, 31-111 Kraków
www.pwm.com.pl

Wyd. I. Printed in Poland 2023. Drukarnia REGIS Sp. z
o.o ul. Napoleona 4, 05-230 Kobyłka

ISBN 83-87202-84-3

FRYDERYK CHOPIN
CONCERTO in F minor Op. 21
version for one piano

Performance Commentary
Source Commentary (abridged)

PERFORMANCE COMMENTARY

Introductory remarks

During Chopin's lifetime piano concertos were performed in four versions:
1. The version for one piano. This editorial form, fundamental at the time, of compositions for the piano with an orchestra accompaniment – solo piano in normal print, *tutti* and certain soli of orchestral instruments in smaller print – was also a form of presenting the work in salons and even concert halls, as evidenced by the author's printed variants to be applied "in execution without accompaniment", occurring in Chopin's smaller concert works (Op. 2, 14) and a harmonic accompaniment to the recitative in the second movement of the *Concerto,* written by the composer in a pupil's copy (bars 45-72, cf. *Source Commentary*). We cannot exclude the possibility that Chopin himself performed in public the version for one piano of the *Concerto in E minor*, Op. 11.
Orchestral parts supplemented the printed form of this version. It was possible to purchase a complete set for full orchestra or quintet parts only.
2. The version with a second piano was used while playing at home, during lessons and sometimes at public concerts. Wilhelm von Lenz, Chopin's pupil, described the performance of the first movement of the *Concerto in E minor* Op. 11 given by another pupil, Carl Filtsch, accompanied by the composer himself: "Chopin recreated the whole well-devised, ephemeral instrumentation of this composition in his incomparable accompaniment. He played by heart. Never before have I heard anything to equal the first *tutti*, performed by him on the piano"[1].
However, piano reductions of the orchestra part in Chopin's *Concertos* were not published until about 1860. Earlier, use was made of handwritten reductions (extant reductions of the second and third movement of both *Concertos* were made by Chopin's friends J. Fontana and A. Franchomme). Owing to the fact that the *Concerto* was not published in this version during the composer's lifetime, the *National Edition* presents it in series B.
3. The version with a string quartet (quintet) was used both during concerts and in salons. In 1829, Chopin wrote to T. Woyciechowski: "Every Friday Kessler holds small musical meetings [...] A fortnight ago, there was Ries' *Concerto* in a quartet", and a year later he mentioned preparations for a performance of his *Concerto in E minor* Op. 11: "Last Wednesday I rehearsed my *Concerto* in a quartet".
4. The composer intended the version with the orchestra to be the basic one. On 17 March 1830, he performed the *Concerto in F minor* in Warsaw in this version (see quotations *about the Concerto...* prior to the musical text). Chopin prepared the base for printing the *Concerto in F minor* in the form of a handwritten score of precisely this version (cf. a characteristic of sources in the *Source Commentary*).

Notes on the musical text

The variants marked as *ossia* were given this label by Chopin or were added in his hand to pupils' copies; variants without this designation are the result of discrepancies in the texts of authentic versions or an inability to establish an unambiguous reading of the text.
Minor authentic alternatives (single notes, ornaments, slurs, accents, pedal indications, etc.) that can be regarded as variants are enclosed in round brackets ( ), whilst editorial additions are written in square brackets [].
Pianists who are not interested in editorial questions, and want to base their performance on a single text, unhampered by variants, are recommended to use the music printed in the principal staves, including all the markings in brackets.
Chopin's original fingering is indicated in large bold-type numerals, **1 2 3 4 5**, in contrast to the editors' fingering which is written in small italic numerals, *1 2 3 4 5*. Wherever authentic fingering is enclosed in parentheses this means that it was not present in the primary sources, but added by Chopin to his pupils' copies. The dashed signs indicating the distribution of parts between the hands come from the editors.
A general discussion on the interpretation of Chopin's works is to be contained in a separate volume: *The Introduction to the National Edition*, in the section entitled *Problems of Performance*.

Abbreviations: R.H. – right hand, L.H. – left hand.

---

[1] Wilhelm von Lenz, *Uebersichtliche Beurtheilung der Pianoforte-Kompositionen von Chopin [...]*, "Neue Berliner Musikzeitung" 4 September 1872.

Concerto in F minor Op. 21

Attention should be drawn to the proper realisation of the authentic slurring. Short slurs, characteristic for this period in Chopin's oeuvre, usually do not encompass whole phrases – the beginnings of the slurs should be accentuated by delicate pressure, but the player should be warned against lifting the hand when the end of a slur occurs within a phrase.
In general, the realisation of individual grace-notes does not pose a problem: in the majority of cases, it is unessential whether the grace-note is executed in an anticipatory manner or – in accordance with classical rules – on the downbeat; it is only important that it be played as quickly as possible and with distinct articulation. Situations in which one of the above possibilities appears to be clearly closer to Chopin's style are discussed below in commentaries to particular bars.

I. Maestoso

p. 12 *Bar 72* The trill should be started from the main note.

p. 13 *Bar 79 and 80* The arpeggio notation in the form of separate wavy lines for each hand does not determine the manner of their realisation. They can be rendered continuously (1) or simultaneously in both hands (2). The editors recommend arpeggiation only in the L.H. (3), which grants the chords a more decisive character without losing the impression of an arpeggio.

Bar 87 R.H. Beginning of the trill with a grace-note:

 (main text),

(variant).

In each of the above solutions the first note should be struck simultaneously with *d♭* in the L.H.

p. 14 *Bar 95* R.H. Beginning of the trill with grace-notes:

 ; *e¹* simultaneously with *d* in the L.H.

Bar 97 R.H. Beginning of the trill:

p. 15 *Bar 112* R.H. The editors recommend playing the last semiquaver with the first finger, which is very comfortable and dependable when applying the following device:

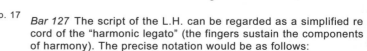

p. 17 *Bar 127* The script of the L.H. can be regarded as a simplified record of the "harmonic legato" (the fingers sustain the components of harmony). The precise notation would be as follows:

(similarly in bar 275).

Bar 128 R.H. The grace-note *g²* should be played together with the third quaver in the L.H. The graphic form of this grace-note (an uncrossed quaver) does not render precise its rhythmic value. It can be performed as an ordinary crossed grace-note or slightly longer, e. g. in the manner noted by Chopin in analogous bar 276.

Bar 132 and 280 R.H. Taking into account the arpeggio, it should be performed in accordance with the following scheme:

p. 19 *Bars 165-168 and 315-318* Easier fingering in bars 165-166:

(the note *bb*, the eighth semiquaver in bar 166, can be played in the L.H. or R.H.); analogously in bars 167-168.
Bar 315 and 317 can be performed similarly:

p. 20 *Bars 179-180 and 335-336* In the opinion of the editors the signs *tr* occurring in the notation of the R.H. part mean that the whole combination of the trill and tremolando can be played not only in semiquavers, but also freely, with a speed adapted to the accepted tempo of this fragment and the performance skills of the pianist.

p. 22 *Bar 208* R.H. Proposal of solving the beginning of the bar:

p. 27 *Bar 272* R.H.  The lower note of the arpeggio, *d¹*, should be struck simultaneously with *cb¹* in the L.H.

p. 28 *Bars 297-298* Notes written in a smaller typeface on the lower staff are only an illustration of the harmonic progression of the orchestra accompaniment. In no case they should be played.

p. 30 *Bar 321* Facilitation for smaller hand:

II. Larghetto

p. 32 *Bar 7, 10, 25, 29, 39, 63, 70, 78* R.H. Beginning of the trill with grace-notes in bar 7:  ; *d³* should be played simultaneously with the chord in the L.H.
Analogously in remaining bars.

p. 33 *Bar 28* R.H. The first in the group of small notes in the middle of the bar (*a¹*) should be struck together with *Bb₁* in the L.H., as was marked by Chopin in a pupil's copy in analogous bar 9.

Bars 42 and 43 In the performance of the solo version of the *Concerto* (without accompaniment) the octaves *Eb-eb*, which begin the passages on the fourth beat, should be played in the L.H. Similarly octaves *Ab₁-Ab* in the beginning of bar 43 and 44.

p. 35 *Bar 52* R.H. Chopin clearly distinguished the staccato signs in the autograph by writing wedges instead of dots above the notes *eb* and *bb*. He probably had in mind a more acute distinction of these two sounds.

p. 38 *Bar 76* R.H. Beginning of trill with a grace-note:

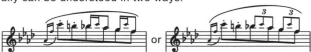

In both cases, the first note should be struck simultaneously with the chord in the L.H.

Bar 77 R.H. Chopin's fingering – number 1 written twice next to *bb¹* and *db²* – is not supposed to denote a simultaneous striking of the two keys with one finger, but their consecutive execution conceived as a beginning of the arpeggiated five-note chord.

Bar 80 This bar can be played in three ways (cf. *Source commentary*):
— as in the main text;
— taking into consideration variants in both hands parts;
— in the manner described in the footnote, which in practice means that the main text is supplemented with the note *c²* which fills chromatic progression on the third quaver in the bar.

III. Allegro vivace

p. 40 *Bar 27 and 335* R.H. Rhythmic notation used by Chopin theoretically can be understood in two ways:

In practice the most important is a smooth rendition of thematic bottom voice.

p. 41 *Bars 37-40 molto legato* means here certainly "harmonic legato" (the fingers sustain the components of harmony). Part of each hand should be therefore treated in a two-part manner:

p. 42 *Bar 71 and 79* R.H. Beginning of the trill: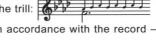

In bar 71 this figure should be – in accordance with the record – preceded by the grace-note *ab¹*.

p. 49 *Bar 246 and 250*

p. 55 *Bars 403-409 and 491-494* R.H. In these bars attention is drawn to the absence of agogic markings. This probably means that Chopin envisaged them played without restraining the natural course of music by slowing down in bars 403-405 and 491-492, as is generally the case in the contemporary performance practice. Thus, the editors recommend the retention of a uniform tempo in these bars. In the second of the discussed passages this could enhance the effect caused by the general pause in bar 493. (Cf. commentary to bars 388-409 in concert version of the score.)

Bar 412 R.H.

p. 59 *t. 491* Possible realisations of arpeggios – see commentary to the first movement, bar 79 and 80.

Bars 511-514 In the opinion of the editors the whole ending (from the first chord in bar 511) can be included into the solo part.

Jan Ekier, Paweł Kamiński

SOURCE COMMENTARY /ABRIDGED/

Introductory comments

The following commentary pertains to the piano part, encompassing, apart from the solo part, also Chopin's piano reduction of the orchestral fragments. The commentary sets out in an abridged form the principles of editing the musical text and discusses the most important discrepancies between the authentic sources; furthermore, it draws attention to departures from the authentic text which are most frequently encountered in the collected editions of Chopin's music compiled after his death. A commentary concerning the whole orchestra part is added to the score of the *Concerto*.

A separately published *Source Commentary* contains a detailed description of the sources, their filiation, justification of the choice of primary sources, a thorough presentation of the differences between them and a reproduction of characteristic fragments.

Abbreviations: R.H. – right hand, L.H. – left hand. The sign → symbolises a connection between sources; it should be read "and... based on it".

Order of the Concertos

The titular issue calls for additional explanation in view of the inconsistency between the order of the origin of both *Concertos*, their performance by Chopin and their publication.

First mention of the *Concertos* was made in Chopin's correspondence in October 1829, in which the composer described the *Concerto in F minor* simply as "my concerto". Its first performance, with Chopin as the soloist, took place on 17 March 1830 in the National Theatre in Warsaw (see quotations *about the Concerto in F minor...* prior to the musical text). From April 1830, Chopin already wrote about his "new" or "second concerto" by which he meant the *Concerto in E minor* (cf. quotations prior to the musical text of *Concerto in E minor*). The première of this work took place on 11 October 1830, also in the National Theatre.

In view of the date of origin and the first performance the rank of the first *Concerto* is thus due to the *Concerto in F minor*.

After his arrival in Paris, Chopin gave several public performances of the *Concerto in E minor* in 1832-1833. The success of those presentations contributed directly to stirring the interest of the publishers. It is not surprising, therefore, that it was precisely the *Concerto in E minor* which was among the first group of compositions (Op. 6-11) issued in Paris in the first half of 1833 (they were also published at a close date in Leipzig and London). The marketing calculations of M. Schlesinger, Chopin's prime Parisian publisher, were decisive for delaying the publication of the *Concerto in F minor* until 1836.

Already while preparing the handwritten bases for the publishers Chopin took into consideration the sequence created by the dates of publication; hence, the autograph of the piano reduction of the *Tutti* opening the *Concerto in E minor* is entitled "1er Concerto" and the semi-autograph of the score of the *Concerto in F minor* – "2d Concerto" (these are the only preserved autographs of the *Concertos*).

The sequence perpetuated in the editions and stemming from the dates of publication and the associated opus numeration contradicts, therefore, the chronology of the origin of the *Concertos*, which is of essential significance both for research dealing with Chopin's oeuvre and certain aspects of performance. Taking these facts into consideration the editors of the *National Edition* decided to omit the reference numbers in the titles, and left only the key and the number of the opus for the purposes of identifying the *Concertos*.

Concerto in F minor, Opus 21

Sources
As   Sketch autograph of a one-and-a-half bar long fragment of the first movement of the *Concerto* (written together with several other unconnected sketches on the last page of the autograph of *Trio* Op. 8; Chopin Society, Warsaw). It encompasses the full record of bar 225 arranged for two pianos and an outline of the further sequence.

[SI]   Lost manuscript of the *Concerto* score, probably an autograph, completed in Warsaw (possibly at the beginning of 1830). [SI] comprised a point of departure for the extant semi-autograph of the score, and in all likelihood served Julian Fontana for editing the piano reduction of the orchestra part.

½A   Semi-autograph of the *Concerto* score (National Library, Warsaw), prepared by Chopin together with an unknown copyist as the basis for the first German edition, probably at the turn of 1835. Chopin wrote the whole solo part and a decisive majority of the supplementary piano reduction of the purely orchestral fragments as well as the title page, the metronomic tempi and a number of supplements and corrections in the orchestral parts. The copyist wrote – possibly upon the basis of [SI] – parts of the orchestral instruments and presumably fragments of the piano reduction of several *Tutti* (only in the second and third movement; in some cases the copyist most probably thickened the text delicately marked by Chopin).

Characteristically, fragments of the orchestra part, which can be recreated upon the basis of the piano part (predominantly the so-called *Tutti*), differ as regards certain details from the version stemming from the parts of orchestral instruments.

Later on (about 1860) – ½A was used also for editing the second German edition and the first edition of the *Concerto* score (Breitkopf & Härtel, Leipzig, no. 10721); some of the supplements, also in the solo piano part (e. g. accidentals in first movement, bars 316, 322 and 324), could originate from this period.

The piano part in ½A was prepared by Chopin extremely carefully as evidenced by the great variety and precision of performance markings as well as the numerous corrections (scratching and deletions). Haste, growing in the course of writing, is discernible especially in the record of the third movement of the *Concerto*. Numerous imprecision in the notation of the accidentals (characteristic especially in Chopin's earlier compositions) as a rule does not hamper a correct deciphering of the text.

A, M^{orch}   – piano part and parts of orchestral instruments in ½A, constituting Chopin's autograph and a manuscript by an unknown copyist (with annotations by Chopin), respectively.

ReF   manuscript of a piano reduction of the orchestra part of the second and third movement of the *Concerto* (lost, photocopy in the Archive of New Acts, Warsaw), made by Julian Fontana most probably upon the basis of [SI]. In the longer fragments, marked as *Tutti* and played by the orchestra alone, Fontana possibly copied the original edition of Chopin's piano reduction contained in [SI]. Some of the pencilled annotations testify to the fact that the manuscript was used for practical purposes, most likely by Fontana himself.

GE1   First German edition, Breitkopf & Härtel (5654), Leipzig March 1836, encompassing the *Concerto* in a version for solo piano and orchestral parts. GE1 is based on ½A, as evidenced by:
— the concurrence of the texts of both sources (more serious doubts are produced only by the slurring, discussed below);
— the storage of ½A in the Breitkopf & Härtel archives;
— more than ten signs visible in ½A possibly added by the engraver of this edition and corresponding to the endings of the pages of the piano part in GE1;
— several places in which the concurrent text of the editions is a modification of the script of A (primarily the supplementation of the missing accidentals); traces of an introduction of those changes can be perceived in GE1 and are absent in the remaining editions.

Piano part in GE1 contains traces of detailed proofreading. Only some of the introduced alterations can be unreservedly ascribed to Chopin (e.g. first movement, bar 224, second movement, bar 28, and third movement, bars 366 and 368), and the majority is probably the work of a reviser. Some errors remained uncorrected.

Separate discussion is due to the s l u r r i n g which in GE1 differs greatly from the slurring in A (e. g. first movement, bars 31-34, 225-228, 300, second movement, bars 15-23, third movement, bars 29-31). A precise analysis, especially of the state prior to the proofreading which can be recreated upon the basis of the visible traces of changes on the plates (more than a hundred), leads to the following conclusions:

— unfamiliar with Chopin's manner of writing the slurs (which in the composer's autographs e n c o m p a s s, contrary to the universally accepted convention, the first and the last note, as in our edition), the engraver of **GE**1 frequently did not understand their meaning and was unable to properly place the beginnings and endings of the slurs;

— the slurring printed originally in **GE**1 frequently corresponds to the habits of the engraver rather than recreates the notation in **A** (the most frequent alterations include: adapting the slurs to the metric structures, especially half-bars and whole bars, the avoidance of excessively long slurs, the addition of slurs in adjoining or analogous figures, e. g. in the second hand);

— the proof-reading, certainly made upon the initiative of Chopin and partially under his control, as a rule restored the slurring from **A**; a considerable number of the alterations, however, remained uncorrected.

GE1a – later impressions of **GE**1, after 1840, with a changed price on the cover and containing solely slight graphical retouching.

GE = **GE**1 and **GE**1a.

GEpiano, **GE**orch – piano part and orchestral parts from **GE**; these symbols are used only in those cases when 'GE' alone could lead to vagueness. The editors of the National Edition had at their disposal a single copy of the parts; thus it was impossible to describe its affiliation to **GE**1 or **GE**1a. Nonetheless, the existence of different impressions of the orchestral material in **GE** appears to be rather unlikely.

GE2 Second German edition (same firm and number), about 1860, thoroughly revised, mainly in comparison with **A** (**A** versions have been restored in several places even in those cases when the alterations in **GE**1 were probably made by Chopin). The alterations encompassed the pitch and rhythmic text, and predominantly the dynamic and articulation markings, including slurring. Furthermore, this edition revised the accidentals, corrected errors (also those taken from **A**, not always aptly), and altered the layout of the text on the staves and pages. Edited after Chopin's death, **GE**2 does not influence the determination of the text; we discuss versions of this edition only in the most important cases. There are copies of **GE**2 with different prices on the cover.

FE First French edition, M. Schlesinger (M.S.1940), Paris, encompassing the *Concerto* in a version for solo piano and orchestral parts:

FE1 First impression of **FE**, August 1836, based on **GE**1 and corrected by Chopin. This edition contains a large number of mistakes concerning the pitch, accidentals, etc. (some had been taken from **GE**1).

FE2 Second impression of **FE** (same firm and number), prepared soon after the first edition and containing about 30 corrections, primarily of pitch errors. It is very possible that Chopin participated in the proofreading of **FE**2, which was probably carried out in two phases (cf. the characteristic of **EE** proposed below). There are copies of **FE**2 different only as regards details of covers, i. a. prices, originating from impressions by Brandus, Schlesinger's successor.

FEpiano (**FE**1piano, **FE**2piano), **FE**orch – piano part and orchestral parts from **FE** (analogous to **GE**piano, **GE**orch). The editors of the National Edition saw only the parts of the first and second violins and the viola (one copy each); upon this basis it is impossible to determine the impression from which those parts originate, and whether there were any different impressions of the **FE** orchestral material.

FED, **FE**S – pupil's copies of **FE**2piano with annotations by Chopin:
  FED – copy from a collection belonging to Chopin's pupil Camille Dubois (Bibliothèque Nationale, Paris), containing fingering, performance directives and corrected printing errors;
  FES – copy from a collection belonging to Chopin's pupil Jane Stirling (Bibliothèque Nationale, Paris), containing amended errors, fingering and predominantly a different version of the middle section of the second movement to be used in a solo performance, in which the recitative (the upper line performed with the right hand) is supplemented with a figurate harmonic accompaniment.

FEJ copy of **FE**2piano from a collection belonging to Chopin's sister, Ludwika Jędrzejewiczowa (Chopin Society, Warsaw), containing pencilled corrections of several errors.

EE First English edition, Wessel & Co (W & Cº Nº 1642), London November 1836, encompassing the *Concerto* in a version for solo piano (the orchestral parts were not printed by Wessel). **EE** is based most probably on a copy of **FE**2 which does not contain several last retouches and was carefully revised by the publisher. Nothing indicates that Chopin participated in its preparation.

E d i t o r i a l   p r i n c i p l e s   f o r   t h e   s o l o   p a r t
We accept **A** as the basis, and take into consideration later changes in **GE** and **FE** according to the following principles:
— we give the corrections of **A** version, made unquestionably by Chopin and introduced in these editions, as the only text;
— whenever Chopin corrected a text published with errors we give the amended version in the main text, and version **A** – in the variant;
— whenever Chopin wavered between two versions we give both, one in the main text and the other as a variant;
— we also give variants when the **GE** or **FE** version can be ascribed, with lesser or greater probability, to Chopin, but there is no distinct proof of its authenticity.
We also take into consideration Chopin's annotations in **FE**D and **FE**S.

I. Maestoso

R e d u c t i o n   o f   t h e   o r c h e s t r a   p a r t
p. 10
Beginning **GE** (→**FE**→**EE**) has mistakenly **c** as the time signature. Errors of this sort were often committed in Chopin's works, e. g. in five out of the six *Etudes* from Op. 25, maintained in the **¢** metre.

Bars 1-70 In **GE** the whole first *Tutti* is erroneously written in notes of normal size.

p. 11
Bars 39-40 R.H. In **A** the slur runs from the middle of bar 39 to the dotted crotchet eb^2 in bar 40. In **GE** it begins a crotchet earlier. In **FE**(→**EE**) the slur taken from **GE** was prolonged up to e^2 in bar 40. Since this change, made probably in the proofs of **FE**1, could have been introduced by Chopin, we give the slur from **FE**.

Bar 46 L.H. The beginning of the bar in **GE** (→**FE**→**EE**) omits the grace note Eb. We add the lower Ab in the middle of the bar as an analogy to bar 134 and 282.

T h e   s o l o   p a r t
p. 12
Bars 71-72 **GE** (→**FE**→**EE**) omits pedal markings.

p. 13
Bars 77-78 R.H. In **GE** (→**FF**→**EE**) the first part of the slur beginning on the fourth crotchet in bar 77 (this bar ends the page in ½**A**) was mistakenly deciphered as a tie sustaining f^1. (Cf. beginning of bar 4 where an accent was placed above a repeated f^1).

Bar 81 R.H. Some of the later collected editions arbitrarily reduced the first note ab^3 on the third beat to the value of a demisemiquaver. We leave the rhythmically undefined notation from the sources since it does not give rise to doubts concerning the manner of performing this figure, and most probably does not contain an error – it could be understood as [music notation] or [music notation].

Bar 84 L.H. The first quaver in **GE** (→**FE**→**EE**) is mistakenly the *c-e* third. Chopin corrected this error in **FE**D.

Bar 85 R.H. In the sources the slur is interrupted in the middle of the bar. In **A** the slurs initially encompassed only irregular rhythmic groups on the fourth beat of bar 84 and in the second half of bar 85. Chopin then prolonged the first slur, but did not extend it to the beginning of the second one. In an analogous situation in **A** the slurs in bars 92-93 were linked in a manner which does not produce any doubts. (Cf. also slurs in bar 83 and 91).

Bar 87 R.H. The main text comes from **GE** (→**FE**→**EE**), and the variant from **A**. We do not know whether the change in the pitch of the grace-note is the result of Chopin's proofreading or the carelessness of the engraver, but the fingering written by Chopin in **FE**D testifies to his acceptance of this version. Cf. second movement, bar 76.

Bar 89 R.H. In the main text we give the **A** rhythm which does not give rise to source or musical doubts. The version in the footnote comes from **GE** (→**FE**→**EE**). The error most probably committed by the engraver is evidenced by:
— the arrangement of the text in **GE**, which excludes the possibility of correcting the rhythm in this place;
— the unnatural character of the dotted rhythm on the third beat combined with authentic phrasing (cf. the previous bar).
The sign written by Chopin in **FE**D (a cross characteristic for pupil's copies) testifies to some sort of spoken remarks made by the composer which could have pertained to the rhythm.

Bar 90 R.H. In **GE** the *staccato* dots for the lower voice, visible in **A**, were omitted possibly to due to carelessness and then supplemented in **FE** (→**EE**).

p. 14   *Bar 93* R.H. In the second half of the bar we leave rhythmic notation from the sources, in which the run is written in semi-quavers (except the last note). Chopin frequently used this type of script, which probably contained a suggestion concerning a *poco ritenuto* performance of this figure. Cf. second movement, bar 41, and, e. g. *Prélude in D♭* Op. 28 no. 15, bar 4 and 79.
L.H. In the sources both notes of the *f-a♭* third on the fourth beat have the value of a semiquaver. Cf. analogous bar 83, 85 and 91.

Bar 96 In **A** (→**GE**→**FE**) the sign ℘ is placed above the R.H. since the purpose of depressing the pedal is predominantly to retain the sound of the minim g^2. Chopin used a similar script in *Prélude in F♯* Op. 28 no. 13, bars 33-35.
In **FE**D Chopin added the sign assigning f^1 to the fourth beat to the L.H.

Bar 98 L.H. In **A** there are no stems prolonging *a♭* and f^1 on the first and fourth beat nor the note c^2 on the seventh quaver. Those elements were supplemented in **GE** (→**FE**). In the proofs of **FE** (→**EE**) Chopin added to the **GE** version a tie sustaining c^2. The supplements partially eliminate the distinct gap in the continuous rendition of the bass line in this phrase (with the help of a prolongation of suitable notes and the pedal). This is the reason why we suggest prolonging also the remaining two bass notes.
R.H. In **FE**D Chopin added *staccato* marking above the fifth on the second beat.

Bar 100 R.H. **A** lacks naturals rising *d♭* to *d* (they are found in the L.H.). This imprecision was only partially corrected in **GE** (→**FE**) by adding ♮ before the second semiquaver in the third group.

Bar 103 L.H. In **A** there are no naturals before the fourth and fifth semiquaver. In **GE** (→**FE**) they were mistakenly added before the third and fourth note.

p. 15   *Bar 105 and 107* L.H. The sources lack ♮ restoring *f* on the seventh quaver in bar 105. Similarly, in bar 107 Chopin overlooked ♮ before f^1.

Bars 108-109 L.H. In the sources there is no tie sustaining c^1. This is probably a Chopin's oversight – cf. analogous bars 106-107 and the note, made below, concerning the R.H.
R.H. **A** (→**GE**→**FE**1) does not have a tie sustaining bb^2. Chopin added it in the proofs of **FE**2 (→**EE**).

Bar 109 L.H. In the last chord **GE** has an additional note c^1. In **FE** (→**EE**) Chopin corrected this mistake.

Bar 109 and 110 R.H. In **A** the thirteenth semiquaver in both bars does not have ♭ restoring db^2. The signs were added in the proofs of **GE** (→**FE**→**EE**).

Bars 110-111 L.H. It is not clear whether Chopin wished to sustain or repeat *f* at the beginning of bar 111:
— there is no tie in **A**, but this could be an oversight (bar 111 starts a new page; in bars 109-110 *f* is sustained in an almost identical context);
— the tie is present in **FE** (→**EE**), but its authenticity can be questioned (the engraver of **FE** could have in this manner interpreted the slur in **GE**, of unclear purpose and spanning from *g* in the last chord of bar 110 to one of the bottom notes in the first chord of bar 111, and possibly constituting a deformed slur, which in **A** is written above those chords).

Bar 111 In **FE** (→**EE**) both ***f*** signs are omitted.
L.H. In **A** the slur ends on the penultimate quaver, and in **GE** (→**FE**→**EE**) – on the last one. This change is probably accidental, but the fingering added later by Chopin – on the last quaver in the proofs of **FE** (→**EE**), on the first sixth in **FE**D – enjoins to recognise this slur as accepted by the composer.

Bar 112 R.H. The fingering above the last two semiquavers is written in **FE**D. The **2** above ab^2 was most probably replaced by **1**, while the result of alterations concerning the same figures above f^3 remains uncertain.

Bar 113 **FE**D contains Chopin's unclear annotation discussed in the footnote.

p. 16   *Bar 119 and 120* R.H. The sources lack ♮ restoring f^3 on the twelfth semiquaver in bar 119 and f^2 in bar 120.

Bar 120 R.H. The sign ∿ above the fourth semiquaver is found only in **A**. We do not know whether its absence in **GE** (→**FE**→**EE**) is the result of Chopin's proofreading or the carelessness of the engraver.

Bar 121 L.H. **GE** (→**FE**→**EE**) has mistakenly ***p*** instead of ℘ before the chord on the third crotchet. Cf. commentary to bar 283.

p. 17   *Bar 127* R.H. **GE** (→**FE**→**EE**) omitted eb^2, the eighth note of the run.

Bar 132 L.H. Some of the later collected editions arbitrarily added the upper octave *e♭* to the authentic *E♭* on the fourth beat. See commentary to bar 280.

Bar 132 and 280 R.H. In **FE**D Chopin added arpeggios at the beginning of those bars.

Bar 133 R.H. The marking *ten.* was added by Chopin in **FE**D.

Bar 135 and 283 L.H. In both bars in **A** (→**GE**) the note *e♭*, sustained from the earlier bar, has the value of a crotchet. In the proofs of **FE** (→**EE**) Chopin changed it in bar 135 into a dotted minim, which should be accepted also in bar 283 (the omission of one of several recurring fragments while introducing corrections is one of his most frequent mistakes).

Bar 138 R.H. **FE** (→**EE**) omitted ♭ prior to the first note of the melody.
L.H. In the proofs of **FE** (→**EE**) Chopin added the marking *sempre legato* and the pedalling.

Bar 138 and 286 R.H. In the proofs of **FE** (→**EE**) Chopin added the tie sustaining eb^2 in the second half of bar 138. This is a characteristic Chopinesque execution device guaranteeing a strict legato of the melody led in chords (cf. e. g. *Polonaise in A♭* Op. 53, bar 97). This alteration can be also applied in bar 286 (see above commentary to bar 135 and 283).

Bar 139 R.H. In **FE** (→**EE**) the first half of the bar has the following mistaken form: . In **FE**D Chopin amended the majority of errors, restoring the **A** version (with the exception of a mordent on the first note).

Bar 139 and 287 R.H. In **A** there is no ♭ restoring db^2 on the penultimate quaver. Chopin corrected the error in bar 287 in the proofs of **GE** (→**FE**→**EE**), and in bar 139 – only in **FE**D.

Bars 139-140 R.H. The *staccato* dots in **GE** (→**FE**→**EE**) were mistakenly assigned (contrary to **A**) also to the first notes in both bars and the four last semiquavers in bar 140.

Bar 140 R.H. **FE** omitted ♮ prior to the second semiquaver. In **EE** this version was mistakenly revised by adding ♭ before this note.

p. 18

Bar 141 L.H. In this bar **A** has six *staccato* dots, overlooked in **GE**. In the proofs of **FE** (→**EE**) Chopin added the dots, but only next to the bass notes, as in bar 289.

Bar 142 L.H. There are no articulation markings in **A** (→**GE**). In the proofs of **FE** (→**EE**) Chopin added a dot and a slur.
R.H. The tie sustaining the minim ab^1 is present in **A** (→**GE**→**FE**→**EE**). We should not exclude the possibility that Chopin deleted the tie while adding a note in **FE**D (see below).
R.H. In **GE** (→**FE**→**EE**) the crotchet eb^1 in the bottom voice was omitted in the middle of the bar. Chopin added it in **FE**D.

Bar 143 L.H. The first quaver in **GE** (→**FE**1) is *G*. Chopin corrected this mistake in the proofs of **FE**2 (→**EE**).
R.H. The sources lack ♯ before the penultimate note. In this type of figures transferred by an octave Chopin frequently did not repeat accidentals, which he regarded as obvious. The fact that he heard $f\#^2$ is testified by ♮ added in the proofs of **FE** (→**EE**) before the f^1-f^2 octave in the following bar.

Bar 144 L. In the proofs of **FE** (→**EE**) Chopin added stems prolonging *c* on the second and sixth quaver.

Bar 146 R.H. **A** has the sign ⟍ above the second half of the bar. Instead of it, **GE** (→**FE** →**EE**) has the marking *cresc.* between the staves, between the fifth and sixth quaver of the bar. In **FE**D Chopin transferred this marking further, which we accept in our edition.

Bars 147-148 **GE** (→**FE**→**EE**) overlooked the marking *cresc.* - - -.

Bar 148 R.H. In the proofs of **FE** (→**EE**) Chopin added a fermata above the crotchet c^4.

Bar 151, 153 and 155 Signs *f* and *p* were written in **FE**D. The signs in bar 151 and 155 are unclear, but combined with the incontestable *p* in bar 153 deciphering them as *f* appears to be highly probable.

Bar 151, 153, 155 and 157 R.H. On the first semiquavers **A** has signs *tr* in bar 151 and 153, and ⤳ in bar 155 and 157 (in this context, these signs are equivalent). In **GE** *tr* was mistakenly deciphered also in bar 155. In the proofs of **FE** (→**EE**) Chopin altered all *tr* into ⤳ (the correction was imprecise, and thus there is no sign in bar 153 in **FE**).

Bars 151-155 ff. In this whole fragment **A** has only one ♮ raising d♭ to d. The majority of the missing signs was added in the proofs of **GE** (→**FE**→**EE**). Owing to the harmonic context, omissions of individual accidentals are encountered also in the successive four bars.

p. 19

Bar 156 and 158 L.H. We give the slurs from **A**. **GE** has half-bar slurs (four or three quavers each). In the proofs of **FE** (→**EE**) Chopin linked the slurs within the bars, leaving the imprecisely marked moment of their beginning, presumably considered less jarring.

Bar 157 L.H. **A** has *F* as the first quaver of the second half of the bar. In the proofs of **GE** (→**FE**→**EE**) Chopin changed it into *D*.

Bar 163 R.H. In **FE** there is no tie sustaining eb^2.

Bar 164 R.H. **A** has an accent above c^3. In **GE** (→**FE**→**EE**) it was placed erroneously a semiquaver later, above the db^2-f^2 third.

Bar 165 and 168 R.H. **A** (→**GE**) has the following version of the third beat in bar 165: [music] and the beginning of bar 168: [music]. In the proofs of **FE** (→**EE**) Chopin, who probably took into consideration the ease of execution, changed c^2 to db^2 in bar 165, and to bb^1 in bar 168. We give this corrected version, analogous to bar 315 and 318, as the only one.

p. 20

Bars 169-170 and 319-320 L.H. In **A** (→**GE**) there are no flats in the second half of the bar, restoring *eb* in bars 169-170 and *ab* in bars 319-320. These errors were amended in the proofs of **FE** (→**EE**).

Bar 171 R.H. In **A** (→**GE**) the slur extends only to the third beat, and the last chord has a *staccato* dot (overlooked in **GE**). We give the longer slur, introduced by Chopin in the proofs of **FE** (→**EE**).

Bar 171 and 321 L.H. In **A** (→**GE**→**FE**) there is no accidental before the 14th semiquaver third from the end in bar 171. **EE** added ♮ raising *Eb* to *E*. The fact that this did not correspond to Chopin's intention is testified by similar bar 321, where in an analogous situation – the absence of the sign in **A** (→**GE**) – *Ab* was restored by adding ♭ in the proofs of **FE** (→**EE**).

Bar 174 L.H. In **GE** (→**FE**→**EE**) the marking *fz* was unnecessarily printed twice, mistakenly placed also at the beginning of the bar.
L.H. The chord on the second beat in **GE** (→**FE**→**EE**) overlooked c^1. In similar contexts Chopin, as a rule, used the arpeggio of a full four-note chord, cf. e. g. *Concerto in E minor* Op. 11, first movement, bar 210, 219 and 570, *Ballade in G minor* Op. 23, bar 124, *Scherzo in Bb minor* Op. 31, bar 470.

Bar 178 L.H. The third semiquaver in **FE** (→**EE**) is *bb* instead of *ab*. This error was corrected in **FE**D and **FE**J.

Reduction of the orchestra part

p. 21

Bar 186 R.H. There is no f^2 on the first quaver in **GE**piano (→**FE**piano→**EE**), possibly due to an oversight.

Bar 187 R.H. The note bb^1 on the fifth quaver of the bottom voice (our main text) occurs in **A** and **M**orch(→**GE**orch→**FE**orch). **GE**piano has a probably mistaken c^2, which in the proofs of **FE**piano (→**EE**) was replaced by the e^1-c^2 sixth. In the footnote we give this version, which topples the consistent harmonic progress in ½**A** as well as being less comfortable from the viewpoint of execution and incompatible with the sound of the orchestra.

Bars 190-197 The dynamic in **A** (→**GE**piano) is arranged differently: *pp* in bar 190, *f* in bar 192, *cresc.* from bar 193 leads only to the second chord in bar 195, which contains *ff*, while bar 197 has *fff* instead of *ff*. We give the simpler dynamic, amended by Chopin in **FE**piano (→**EE**), which, apparently, corresponds better to the sound of the piano.

7

Bars 199-200 R.H. The note g^1 in **GE**piano (→**FE**piano→**EE**) is not sustained, probably due to a misunderstanding of **A**.

Bar 202 L.H. We give the quavers on the second beat as the most probable deciphering of the unclear script in **A**:

. This is concurrent with the rhythm of the first violins in **M**orch (→**GE**orch→**FE**orch). **GE**piano (→**FE**piano→**EE**) has a dotted rhythm, as in the top voice.

Bars 204-205 R.H. The note eb^1 in **GE**piano (→**FE**piano→**EE**) is not sustained, possibly due to a misunderstanding of **A**.

The solo part

p. 22 *Bar 208* R.H. In **FE** (→**EE**) the db^2 appoggiatura was mistakenly placed after a chord. Chopin corrected this error in **FE**D.

Reduction of the orchestra part

Bar 209 R.H. In **A** (**GE**piano→**FE**piano→**EE**) the note bb in the beginning of the bar is a crotchet, probably by mistake.

The solo part

Bar 216 The last three semiquavers in **A** (→**GE**→**FE**) do not have accidentals. This imprecision of the script is characteristic especially for Chopin's earlier compositions.

Bar 219 R.H. In **GE** (→**FE**→**EE**) the sign of the accent was unnecessarily placed also at the beginning of the bar.

p. 23 *Bar 220* L.H. The last two quavers in **A** (→**GE**→**FE**) are cb^1 and d^1. In **EE** this version, incomprehensible from the viewpoint of sonority, was changed – in an analogy to bar 218 – to $c\#^1$-d^1. A similar alteration was introduced in **GE**2 (written as db^1-d^1) and the overwhelming majority of the later collected editions. Strict analogy was not, however, Chopin's intention as testified by his handwritten correction in **FE**D: writing ♮ and ♭, Chopin altered both notes to c^1-db^1. We give this version, which does not produce musical or source doubts, as the only one. In our edition it appears in print for the first time.

Bar 224 R.H. We give the version corrected by Chopin in **GE** (→**FE**→**EE**). Changes of rhythm and articulation visible in **A** make it possible to decipher the two earlier editions of this passage:

(original),

(corrected).

All three versions, which are rather interpretation variants, prove that Chopin sought the most suitable way of performing and recording this passage, and, at the same time, provide an insight into some of the secrets of his *rubato*.

Bar 227 R.H. In **A** (→**GE**→**FE**1) there are no accidentals next to the semiquavers gb and a. In the proofs of **FE**2 flats for gb^2 and gb^3 were added. **EE** lacks these signs, which probably means that they were added in the last phase of the proofreading.

Bar 230 R.H. The eleventh semiquaver in **A** is mistakenly ab, amended in **GE** (→**FE**→**EE**). Another error could be the presence of ab as the fifteenth semiquaver in **FE**. This is the way it was treated in **EE** where it was changed to f. We give the **FE** version as a variant, since Chopin's correction is also possible – ab the penultimate note is reasonably linked with the first chord of the next bar.

p. 24 *Bar 233* L.H. The third group of semiquavers in **FE** has f instead of db. This mistake was corrected in **EE** and **FE**S.

Bar 233 and 235 R.H. Chopin added fingering above the first two semiquavers in the proofs of **FE** (→**EE**).

Bar 234, 236, 238 and 240 L.H. Only **A** has accents below semiquavers written on the upper staff.

Bar 237 **A** (→**GE**→**FE**→**EE**) has fingering in the L.H. on the second beat. Chopin added fingering below the first two semiquavers in the proofs of **FE** (→**EE**) and above them (for the R.H.) in **FE**D.

p. 25 *Bar 247* 𝆑𝅗 occurs in **A**. In **GE** (→**FE**→**EE**) it was mistakenly deciphered as 𝆑.
L.H. The semiquaver third from the end in **GE** is mistakenly f^1, which in **FE** (→**EE**) was corrected to db^1, as in **A**.

Bar 249 **FE** (→**EE**) has erroneously 𝆑 instead of 𝆑𝅗.

Reduction of the orchestra part

p. 26 *Bars 261-267* We give the dynamic markings from **A**. The different markings appearing in **GE**piano (repeated in **FE**piano and **EE**, with the exception of *cresc.* in bar 261) are almost certainly written in a different hand:
— the accidental nature is betrayed by the omission of strokes delineating the range of the *cresc.* from bar 261 and the change of 𝆑𝅗 to 𝆑𝆏 in bar 267;
— 𝆑𝆑𝆑 at the end of bar 265 was most probably wrongly taken from the double bass part in ½**A**;
— alterations of 𝆑𝆑𝆑 to 𝆑𝆑 in bar 264 were made presumably in order to coordinate the preceding *cresc.* with the successive 𝆑𝆑𝆑.

The solo part

p. 27 *Bar 272* R.H. In **A** the arpeggio with grace-notes is written as follows: , which in **GE** was altered to . The notation we accept was introduced by Chopin in the proofs of **FE** (→**EE**). All three scripts certainly denote uniform performance, described in the *Performance Commentary*.

Bar 275 R.H. **GE** (→**FE**→**EE**) overlooked ♮ prior to the second note of the run.
R.H. The sources do not have accidentals before the sixth and tenth note in the run (in accordance with the convention binding in Chopin's time the eventual sign was required only prior to the sixth note). From a formal point of view we should read bb^2 and bb^3, but in upward arpeggios Chopin as a rule used raised passing notes (cf. e. g., bar 87, 95, 143, 175-178, 247-248, 331-334 in this movement), which decisively speaks in favour of b^2 and b^3. We give both possibilities, awarding priority to the version based on the assumption that Chopin's script does not contain an error.

Bar 280 L.H. The main text comes from **A**, and the version given in the footnote is contained in **GE** (→**FE**→**EE**). **GE** does not have any sort of traces of alterations, which suggests a mistake committed by the engraver. The doubling of Eb on the fourth beat appears to be superfluous: the note eb occurs in the cello part, and the introduction of octaves from the first chord in bar 281 subtly accentuates the entrée of the reinforced repetition of the first phrase of the theme. In the appropriate bar of the exposition (bar 132) the note eb does not appear in the solo part in any of the sources.

Bars 282-283 L.H. The tie which in **A** sustains the note eb, in **GE** (→**FE** →**EE**) incorrectly links eb and bb. Cf. bars 134-135.

Bar 283 R.H. The main text comes from **A**, the version in the footnote was introduced in the proofs of **GE** (→**FE**→**EE**). The removal of c^1 gives rise to stylistic doubts – leaving the unresolved db^1 from the first half of the bar deforms the line of the accompanying quaver voice. The fact that the chord on the third beat in **GE** contains visible traces of removing the superfluous note g^2 entitles us to presume that a misunderstanding took place during the correction of some sort of a more serious error. Cf. 135.

L.H. In **GE** (→**FE**→**EE**) the sign 𝄢 was mistakenly deciphered as referring to the ab-eb¹ fifth. Cf. commentary to bar 121.

Bar 285 L.H. The sixth quaver in **FE** (→**EE**) is mistakenly db instead of f.

p. 28   *Bar 287* L.H. The last quaver in **FE** is erroneously g instead of ab.

Bar 290 R.H. The main text comes from **A**, the version in the footnote is contained in **GE** (→**FE**→**EE**). The omission of c² (written in **A** without a precautionary ♮) could be a mistake of the engraver, who repeated the two-voice notation of the melodic notes from the previous bar. Cf. bar 142.

Bar 297 The strings chord recorded on the lower staff in **A** (cf. *Performance Commentary*) was most probably overlooked in **GE**piano (together with the rest following the chord). **FE**piano has an incorrect crotchet G (and rest), which could be a misunderstanding of a correction made by Chopin or a mistakenly printed beginning of the successive bar. **EE** omits the erroneous record in **FE**piano.

p. 29   *Bar 300* R.H. **FE** mistakenly repeated two preceding notes, f¹ and bb¹, on the sixth and seventh semiquaver.

p. 30   *Bar 315* R.H. Some of the later collected editions arbitrarily changed the top note on the tenth semiquaver from gb² to f².

Bar 316 and 324 L.H. **A** contains precautionary ♮ before G at the beginning of those bars. The absence of those signs in **GE** (→**FE**→**EE**) could testify to their later addition in **A** (different handwriting?). Cf. commentary to bar 322.

Bar 318 R.H. Some of the later collected editions arbitrarily altered the top note on the second semiquaver from eb² to f².

Bar 320 R.H. The first chord in **A** is written incorrectly as:

(the dot next to eb² is dubious). We accept a solution analogous to bar 170. In **GE** (→**FE**→**EE**) both notes of the eb²-ab² fourth have the value of a quaver with two dots.

Bar 322 On the first beat **A** has three ♭ lowering g to gb. The absence of those signs in **GE** could indicate their later addition in **A** (cf. commentary to bar 316 and 324). In the proofs of **FE** (→**EE**) all four flats necessary in this bar were added.

p. 31   *Bar 328* In **A** there are no accidentals before the eighth semiquaver in the L.H. and the eleventh semiquaver in the R.H. A flat lowering g² to a gb² on the eighth semiquaver was added in **GE**. In **FE** this sign was probably first placed mistakenly three notes further on, and then both places were suitably amended. **EE** contains the correct version.

Bar 330 R.H. The third semiquaver in **FE** is db, most probably by mistake.

Bar 335 ***ff*** was added by Chopin in the proofs of **FE** (→**EE**). Dynamic markings added at the end of this movement in **FE** can be acknowledged as supplements of the markings in **A**. Cf. commentaries to bar 337, 341 and 345.

Bars 335-336 L.H. In **A** the trilled note is mistakenly c². A similar error, consisting of writing the upper second of the trilled note, which begins the performance of the trill, instead of the trilled note itself was made by Chopin also in *Bolero* Op. 19, bar 187 and *Sonata in Bb minor* Op. 35, second movement, bar 20. In **GE** (→**FE**→**EE**) c² was changed to bb¹ not only in bar 335, but also – possibly due to a misunderstanding – at the beginning of bar 336.

Both parts

Bar 337 ***fz*** and ***ff*** at the beginning of the bar as well as the accent on the second octave in the L.H. come from **A**. They were overlooked in **GE**piano, an error which Chopin corrected only partially in the proofs of **FE**piano (→**EE**) by adding ***f***.

Reduction of the orchestra part

Bar 341 ***p*** and ⟍ were added by Chopin in the proofs of **FE**piano (→**EE**). See commentary to bar 335.

Bar 345 R.H. At the beginning of the bar **A** (→**GE**piano) has f¹ alone. The note ab was added in the proofs of **FE**piano (→**EE**). ***f*** and the accent on the fourth beat are contained in **A**. In **GE**piano the accent was overlooked, and in **FE**piano (→**EE**) the same holds true for ***f***.

Bar 348 R.H. **A** (→**GE**piano) has f¹ alone. Chopin added the note f in the proofs of **FE**piano (→**EE**).

II. Larghetto

Reduction of the orchestra part

p. 32   *Bar 1* **FE**piano overlooked ***pp***. In **FE**S Chopin added ***p***.

Bar 6 R.H. The main text comes from **GE**piano (→**FE**piano→**EE**), the variant from **A**. It seems probable that Chopin took into consideration a performance of this movement without the orchestra accompaniment and resigned from the c¹-ab¹ sixth ending the orchestral introduction (cf. bar 96), although we cannot exclude an oversight committed by the engraver.

The solo part

Bar 6 R.H. In each source the notation of the second half of the bar is different:

Since each script is incorrect from the viewpoint of rhythm it appears doubtful whether we could recognise the version of any of the editions as amended by Chopin. This is the reason why as the point of departure we accept the notation in **A**, removing the second dot prolonging eb¹ (the simplest of all possible corrections, see also commentary to the first movement, bar 320). Owing to the fermata and the improvised and free character of the whole bar, this change has, for all practical purposes, no impact upon execution.

Bar 7, 9, 26 and 75 In **FE**D Chopin added signs enjoining the commencement of the ornament simultaneously with the bass note.

Bar 8 R.H. **A** contains mistaken rhythmic values:

Accepting the natural premise that the slur and the beam of the fourth, fifth and sixth note of the bar denote a semiquaver triplet, we ascertain that the bar consists of nine quavers. The mistake made by Chopin (committed presumably as a consequence of corrections in **A**) can be perceived in the notation of the first, second or last beat:

In **A** the alignment of the R.H. part in relation to the quavers in the L.H. indicates unambiguously that the second of the given schemes is the one which corresponds to Chopin's intention; this is the reason why we give this version as the only one.
GE (→**FE**→**EE**) repeated without any alterations the mistaken rhythmic values from **A**. Nonetheless, they were arranged in such a manner that eight semiquavers uniformly fill the second half of the bar. In **GE2** this version was revised by removing the unnecessary dots prolonging ab^2 to the second beat. This is certainly a misreading since the authentic prolongation dots together with the accent indicate the unquestionably syncopated character of this note.
L.H. On the fifth quaver **FE** (→**EE**) mistakenly contains the additional note c^1. Cf. bar 27 and 76.

Bar 13 and 32 R.H. In **A** the demisemiquaver in both bars is the penultimate note g^3. In bar 32 this version is contained also in **GE**. In bar 13 in **GE** (→**FE**→**EE**) and bar 32 in **FE** (→**EE**) the value of the demisemiquaver was given – most probably as a result of the engravers' errors – to the last note. Cf. commentaries to bar 41 and 81.

Bar 15 L.H. Some of the later collected editions arbitrarily omitted the tie sustaining ab, probably because Chopin did not mark the prolongation of this note in the chord on the third quaver. This sort of simplified script is encountered also in other Chopin's works: *Polonaise in C minor* Op. 40 no. 2, bar 82 and 109 or *Allegro de Concert* Op. 46, bar 162 and 163.

Bar 17 R.H. In **GE** (→**FE**→**EE**) the vertical arc on the fourth beat marking the arpeggio of the c^2-c^3 octave was mistakenly written as encompassing a grace-note, which altered its meaning. This type of script, enjoining a simultaneous sounding of an octave after a grace-note, is contained in the majority of the later collected editions. In some of these editions the grace-note was arbitrarily linked with the bottom note of the octave. Cf. commentary to bar 85.

Bar 18 and 86 R.H. **GE** (→**FE**→**EE**) omitted accents in the form of horizontal strokes perhaps because their application was not yet universal. (Accents of this sort were added by Chopin in a pupil's copy of *Ballade in G minor* Op. 23, bar 194, 196 and 198.)

p. 33
Bar 20 R.H. On the third beat **A** (→**GE**) has the eb^1-ab^1-c^2 chord. Chopin removed ab^1 in the proofs of **FE** (→**EE**).
R.H. In the last chord **GE** contains a^1 instead of c^2. This is most probably a mistake of the engraver, revised by adding ♮. In the proofs of **FE** (→**EE**) Chopin restored the version from **A**.

Bar 21 The main text comes from **A**. **GE** (→**FE**→**EE**) has neither accents nor *dim.*, and the slurs in the R.H. are arranged differently. It is very unlikely that any of those changes was made by Chopin. Nonetheless, in **FE**D he added *pp* on the second quaver of the bar, which should be recognised as at least a partial acceptance of the version from the first editions. We give this supplemented version in the footnote.

Bars 21-22 In **A** the naturals raising db to d do not appear until the fourth crotchet in bar 22, which was corrected in **GE** (→**FE**→**EE**).

Bar 24 R.H. Some of the later collected editions arbitrarily altered the last note from db^3 to f^3.

Bar 25 L.H. The first chord in **A** is mistakenly Eb_1-G_1-Eb-G. Chopin removed Eb_1 in the proofs of **GE** (→**FE**→**EE**). **GE2** gives G_1-Bb_1-Eb-G.

Bar 27 R.H. After the first semiquaver the sources contain a quaver rest. Since the "thrifty" rhythmic notation characteristic for Chopin can, in our opinion, hinder a proper deciphering of the rhythm, we change ǂ to two semiquaver rests.

Bar 28 R.H. In **A** the ornament before db^3 on the second beat amounts to four semiquavers (with two f^1). In the proofs of **GE** (→**FE**→**EE**) Chopin removed the second note, but this was probably a mistakenly engraved ab^1. Hence, Chopin's intention to remove the correct note (f^1) remains uncertain.
R.H. As the second small semiquaver before the passage in the second half of the bar **FE** (→**EE**) mistakenly has c^2 instead of eb^2.

p. 34
Bar 33 and 82 L.H. At the beginning of the bar **A** (→**GE**→**FE**) does not have Eb_1, the bottom note of the octave. Chopin added it in **A** (→**GE**→**FE**→**EE**; in the latter edition it was added also in bar 82) written as *8*, when this phrase first appeared in bar 14. It is most likely that this correction can be applied also in the discussed bars since the omission of one of several recurring fragments while introducing corrections is one of Chopin's frequent mistakes. Cf. commentary to bar 89. It must be kept in mind that while writing the *Concerto* in Warsaw (see *The Order of the Concertos* at the beginning of this commentary) Chopin, practically did not have the note Eb_1 at his disposal because the range of his piano extended only to F_1.

Bar 36 L.H. The graphic distinction of the inner voice of the three last chords with a separate beam comes from the editors. This solution was necessary to mark that it comes precisely this progress that is designated by the sign written by Chopin in **A** between the notes of the chords in a way impossible to recreate in print.

Bar 39 R.H. In **GE** (→**FE**→**EE**) the first grace-note before the trill on the fourth beat is mistakenly ab^2. In **FE**S Chopin restored bb^2, which is found in **A**.

Bar 40 The sign ═══ given in the main text comes from **A**. In **GE** it was placed in the first part of the run, and in **FE** (→**EE**) it was changed to ◁. The shifting of the hairpin in **GE** was, in all likelihood, accidental, but the alteration in **FE** could have been introduced by Chopin, although we cannot exclude the possibility that it is also a mistake committed by the engraver (cf. commentary to *Variations* Op. 12, bar 94). In the footnote we give the version from **FE**.
R.H. The sources do not contain ♭ prior to the last note in the first half of the bar.

Bar 41 R.H. Changes in the pitch of the second note in particular sources testify to Chopin's wavering. **A** has bb^1, **GE** – bbb^1, in the proofs of **FE** (→**EE**) Chopin restored bb^1, and in **FE**D he added bb. This is the reason why we give both versions. The composer's indecision appears to pertain to the fundamental structure of the phrase: the beginning of the bar is melodically connected with the preceding figure containing bbb^1, and harmonically inclines towards the successive chord (on the fourth beat of bar 41), containing bb. A melodic motif tantamount to the variant version Chopin used against the background of a similar harmony in *Mazurka in A minor* Dbop. 42B, bar 52.
L.H. **GE** overlooked cb^1 on the third and fifth quaver of the bar. Chopin corrected this error in the proofs of **FE** (→**EE**).
R.H. We write the figure ending the bar with semiquavers, as in **A** (see commentary to the first movement, bar 93). In **GE** (→**FE**→**EE**) the last note was mistakenly given the value of a demisemiquaver (a reduction of the value of the last note after a rest was frequently encountered in figures of this type – e. g. in bars 37-38 – and could have been conducted by the engraver "automatically", cf. commentaries to bar 81, as well as 13 and 32). The majority of the later collected editions arbitrarily changed the notation of this figure in assorted ways, and usually used the version from the first editions as a point of departure.

p. 35 *Bars 43-44* In the proofs of **FE** (→**EE**) Chopin added flats restoring *B♭* and *b♭* on the fourth beats of the bars. In bar 43 they were mistakenly not placed until the eighth demisemiquaver.

Both parts

Bars 45-72 In **FE**S Chopin wrote a simplified reduction of the orchestra accompaniment to the recitative which could be applied by performing this movement solo. This type of alternative L.H. parts for fragments rendered *unisono* was given by Chopin also in the printed versions of *Variations* Op. 2 and *Krakowiak* Op. 14. In the *Concerto* Chopin replaced the figurate harmonic accompaniment of the original L.H. part as well as supplemented or changed the R.H. part (bar 45, 49-50, 58-60). Despite a simplified and abbreviated notation the deciphering of the added text poses slight difficulties only in several places :
— in bar 45 Chopin wrote the first group of six quavers and marked the successive five figures in bars 45-47 as its repetitions; he was most probably concerned only with repeating the scheme of the harmony and not with a literal repetition of all the notes, since striking upon each occasion the bass in the bottom octave (*As₁*) is inconvenient from the point of view of execution and unjustified as regards sound;
— the second half of bar 60 in the part in the L.H. sketches only the rhythm; this probably means that the *c♭-g♭* fifth should be repeated, as in bar 58;
— over the bar lines of bars 61-62 Chopin did not mark which sounds are to be chosen from the chords on the upper staff; we give the simplest solution;
— in those later collected editions which give the version added in **FE**S bar 62, 66, 70 and 71 contain misreadings of Chopin's notation (*d♭* instead of *c♭* in chords in the second half of bar 62, the absence of the last chord in bar 66, the excessively high position of chords on the second and fourth beat in bar 70, and *B♭* instead of *e♭* as the fundamental bass note in bar 71);
— in bars 64-65 the variant of the accompaniment is a proposal made by the editors, based on the authentic sound of the orchestra recreated according to **Re**F (**M**orch contains a very similar version, but in bar 65 it is recorded with a mistake in the part of the violas).

Reduction of the orchestra part

p. 36 *Bar 61* R.H. In the last chord **GE** (→**FE**→**EE**) has mistakenly the additional note *ab²*.

The solo part

Bar 63 In **FE** (→**EE**) dots prolonging the first quaver are missing in both hands parts.
In some of the later collected editions the grace-notes beginning the trill (in both hands) were arbitrarily repeated as its ending.

p. 37 *Bar 65* Before the sixth semiquaver in the second half of the bar in **A** (→**GE**) there are no ♭ lowering d to *d♭* in both hands. Chopin supplemented them in the proofs of **FE** (→**EE**).

Bar 68 We shift the second quaver slightly to the right, as Chopin wrote in **A**. This notation may signify that he foresaw the rhythm ♩³♪ (in contemporary notation). See commentary to bar 433 and 437 in the third movement of the *Concerto*.

Reduction of the orchestra part

Bar 69 In **A** (→**GE**) the insert of the horns part is written only on the second beat. In the proofs of **FE** (→**EE**) Chopin gave the quaver octave at the beginning.

The solo part

Bar 69 **A** (→**GE**→**FE**) has no ♭ lowering g to *g♭* before the penultimate note in both hands; this is an obvious oversight by Chopin.

Reduction of the orchestra part

Bars 71-72 R.H. In **A** there is no slur over the *f²-ab²* thirds supplementing the trill of the solo part, and the *f²-ab²* third in bar 71 has mistakenly the value of a minim. The slur was added in the proofs of **GE** (→**FE**→**EE**), and the rhythmic error was corrected in **FE** (→**EE**).

The solo part

Bars 72-74 R.H. From the last quaver in bar 72 to the end of bar 74 **A** does not have an *8ᵛᵃ* sign (bar 74 is written an octave lower), so that the whole phrase is written an octave too low.

p. 38 *Bar 76* The main text comes from **A**, the variant – from **GE** (→**FE**→**EE**). We cannot exclude the possibility of Chopin's correction in **GE** (cf. commentary to the first movement, bar 87), but a mistake made by the engraver seems much more probable – cf. analogous bar 8 and 27, where *g²* does not appear until the end of the bar.

Bar 77 R.H. In the proofs of **FE** (→**EE**) Chopin gave the fingering for the first chord.
L.H. **GE** (→**FE**→**EE**) contains the *B♭-g♭* sixth on the sixth quaver. This is the outcome of a misreading of **A**: originally, the stem of *g♭* ended at the level of the note *B♭* (later, Chopin extended it to a beam running below); the end of this stem is characteristically widened (the result of a rapid transference of the pen elsewhere), which the engraver mistakenly took for a note (there are hundreds of such broadening or "hooks" in **A**). Chopin wished to correct this error and mistakenly deleted *g♭* in **FE**S.

Bar 79 R.H. The note *g³* on the fourth quaver in **A** mistakenly has the value of a crotchet.

Bars 79-80 R.H. The repetition or sustaining of *f¹* at the beginning of bar 80 gives rise to doubts since despite a distinct tie this note is accented in **A**. Presumably, Chopin changed his opinion and added one of the markings – the tie or the accent – later, without noticing the resultant vagueness.
The absence of the accent in **GE** (→**FE**→**EE**) could be the outcome of an ordinary oversight and not Chopin's proofreading.

Bar 80 Variants in both hands come from **A** (Chopin mistakenly marked a group of eight notes on the third quaver as a demisemiquaver septimole). In **GE** this version is written with mistakes on the third beat: *d³* (with a superfluous ♮) was repeated as a third semiquaver while ∿ above the fourth semiquaver and the dotted rhythm at the end of this figure were overlooked. The main text comes from **FE** (→**EE**). Changes in the second half of the bar were certainly introduced by Chopin in the proofs of **FE**1, as confirmed by visible traces of corrections in print. On the other hand, traces of this sort cannot be noticed on the third quaver of the bar, making it necessary to take into consideration also the possible omission of *c²* in this figure.
R.H. Only **A** (→**GE**) contains an accent below *f⁴*. It is difficult to say whether in the proofs of **FE** (→**EE**) it was removed or omitted.

p. 39 *Bar 81* R.H. Only **A** has a tie sustaining *c²* at the beginning of the bar. Its absence in **GE** (→**FE**→**EE**) can be explained both as an oversight of the engraver or the result of Chopin's proofreading.
L.H. In the chord on the seventh quaver **GE** (→**FE**→**EE**) overlooked *b♭*. Some of the later collected editions arbitrarily changed the resultant *ab-f¹* sixth to an *ab-db¹* fourth.
R.H. In **A** (→**GE**) the figure closing the bar is as follows:

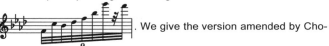

. We give the version amended by Chopin in **FE** (→**EE**). The last note in **GE** (→**FE**→**EE**) is mistakenly written as a hemidemisemiquaver (cf. commentary to bar 41).

Bar 82 R.H. The tie sustaining bb^2 at the beginning of the bar is contained only in **A** (and **GE**2). It is difficult to say whether it was overlooked in **GE** (→**FE**→**EE**) or removed by Chopin in the proofs.

Bar 83 L.H. In the second half of the bar **FE** mistakenly has a c^1-db^1 second.
R.H. **A** erroneously contains an eb^2-c^3 sixth on the fourth beat. **GE** (→**FE**) also mistakenly has a c^2-c^3 octave. Chopin wrote a correct version (analogous to bar 15) into all three extant pupil's copies; it is also in **EE** and **GE**2.

Bar 85 R.H. On the fourth beat **A** has a grace-note and an arpeggio (in the form of a vertical arc), as in bar 17. **GE** omitted the arpeggio sign. The alternative notation of the ornament, given by us, was introduced by the composer in the proofs of **FE** (→**EE**). Both Chopin's scripts denote the same execution.

Bar 87 R.H. f was added by Chopin in **FE**D.
R.H. The last chord in **GE** (→**FE**→**EE**) does not have eb^2. This is most possibly an oversight, cf. bar 19.

Bar 89 Chopin added the marking *appassionato* in the proofs of **FE** (→**EE**).
L.H. The octave at the beginning of the bar – written as 8 – is found only in **A**. Its absence in **GE** (→**FE**→**EE**) is possibly the result of an oversight, although we cannot totally exclude Chopin's proofreading.
L.H. In the penultimate quaver **GE** overlooked c^1. Chopin supplemented the missing note in the proofs of **FE** (→**EE**).

Bar 90 R.H. Chopin wrote a rather illegible annotation more or less on the second quaver of the bar in **FE**D. Presumably, it relates to dynamic, although it is difficult to describe its meaning and purpose.

Reduction of the orchestra part

Bar 93 R.H. **A** (→**GE**) does not contain c^2 at the beginning of the bar. Chopin added this note in the proofs of **FE** (→**EE**).

III. Allegro vivace

The solo part

p. 40
Bars 5-6 L.H. The text from **A** (given by us) was recreated in **GE** (→**FE**) with errors:

(in **EE** the second f^1 was removed). Probably for this reason some later collected editions introduced here the version from analogous bars 329-330.

Bar 11 R.H. At the beginning of the bar **A** contains the grace-note ab^1-f^2 (our variant). Imprecise notation (the absence of a section of the stem linking both notes of the sixth) is the reason why only the upper note f^2 was printed in **GE**. Chopin corrected this mistake in **FE** (→**EE**) in a manner analogous to bar 27, which we accept in the main text.

Reduction of the orchestra part

Bar 19 and 343 R.H. The second note of the melody in **A** (→**GE**^{piano}→**FE**1^{piano}) is eb^2. **M**^{orch} (→**FE**^{orch} →**GE**^{orch}) also has eb^2 in the part of the first violins. In the last phase of proofreading **FE**2 Chopin added naturals raising eb^2 to e^2 (they are absent in **EE**). In **ReF** was added later (in pencil; probably after a comparison with **FE**2^{piano}). In all versions of the *Concerto* we accept the **FE**2^{piano} version amended by Chopin as the last and most likely the final one.

The solo part

Bar 27 In **FE**D Chopin marked the simultaneous sounding of the first grace-note with the bass note.

Bars 30-32 and 374-376 L.H. In **A** chords at the beginning of those bars are recorded in such a way that the dyads of the orchestra accompaniment are distinguished only by smaller script f (in bar 376 Chopin wrote only the solo part note). The different sizes went unnoticed in **GE**, and all the notes of the chords were printed in identical typeface. In **FE** Chopin corrected this error in bars 374-376 by distinguishing even more markedly the solo part from the accompaniment (f) and supplementing the dyad in bar 376 (**FE**1 mistakenly added db^1-f^1, which was amended to c^1-f^1 in **FE**2). **EE** repeated the text from **FE**2, without, however, preserving the different sizes of the notes. All the later collected editions followed the example of **GE** and erroneously included the dyads of the accompaniment into the solo part.

Reduction of the orchestra part

p. 41
Bar 48 R.H. On the second beat **GE**^{piano} (→**FE**1^{piano}) has the ab^1-bb^1-f^2 chord. This mistake was corrected in **FE**2^{piano} (→**EE**).
R.H. On the third beat **A** contains the ab^1-c^2-e^2 chord, an error amended in **GE**^{piano} (→**FE**^{piano}→**EE**).

Bars 63-64 R.H. **A** (→**GE**^{piano}) contains f^1 alone. The note f was added by Chopin in the proofs of **FE**^{piano} (→**EE**).

The solo part

Bar 65 R.H. **A** does not have an 8va sign, a mistake corrected already in **GE** (→**FE**→**EE**).

Bar 68 and 76 On the second beat **A** (→**GE**) has the octave F-f in bar 68 and Eb-eb in bar 76, on the first beat in bar 76 it has Eb. We give the version introduced by Chopin in **FE** (→**EE**).

p. 42
Bar 75 L.H. At the beginning of the bar **A** (→**GE**) has Eb. In the proofs of **FE**1 Chopin changed it to Gb (b indispensable next to this note was not added until **FE**2 (→**EE**)). The majority of the later collected editions arbitrarily introduced the octave Eb_1-Eb with the top note tied to the last Eb in the previous bar (by analogy to bar 67).

Bar 77 L.H. The last chord in **A** (→**GE**) is a-eb^1-gb^1-a^1, and in **FE** (→**EE**) – a-gb^1-a^1. In **FE** the chord was corrected twice (in **FE**1 the bottom note is g), but it remains uncertain whether the removal of eb^1 was the aim of those corrections or the accidental effect of an imprecise amendment of a more serious error.

Bar 78 and 79 We give dynamic markings from **A**. In **GE** (→**FE**→**EE**) p in bar 79 was mistakenly read as f. Moreover, f was added at the beginning of bar 78 (**FE** omitted the accent), which could have been an unfinished attempt at correcting the mistake from bar 79: Chopin could have wished to transfer this marking to bar 78, which was realised "partially" by adding a new sign without removing the old one.

Bars 81-82 L.H. The fingering written by Chopin comes from **A**. **GE** (→**FE** →**EE**) omitted the figures **1** (the one in bar 82 was mistakenly deciphered as a *staccato* dot).

p. 43
Bar 96 **A** does not have the sign ✻. The sign in parentheses comes from **GE** (→**FE**→**EE**); it is uncertain whether it was added by Chopin. The sign in brackets, proposed by the editors, is justified by the authentic pedalling in bars 85-88.

Bars 102-103 R.H. The second and third triplet in bar 102 as well as first and second triplet in bar 103 in **GE** were mistakenly written an octave higher.

p. 44
Bar 113 and 115 R.H. The sources lack ♮ prior to the penultimate notes.

Bar 119 R.H. The penultimate quaver in **A** is g^2 alone. This is most probably an oversight by Chopin, which he amended in **GE** (→**FE**→**EE**).

Bar 124 On the fourth quaver **A** (→**GE**) does not have ♭ lowering *g¹* and *g²* to *g♭¹* and *g♭²*. In the proofs of **FE** (→**EE**) Chopin supplemented them (together with precautionary naturals before g in bar 125).

Reduction of the orchestra part

p. 45
Bars 141-144 L.H. We give the version from **A** (→**GE**piano→**FE**piano →**EE**). In the viola and cello parts the orchestral version – **Re**F, **M**orch (→**GE**orch→**FE**orch) – contains a different rhythmic-articulation solution:

Chopin most probably intentionally differentiated these four bars in the version for the solo piano and with the orchestra by taking into consideration differences in the sound of the piano and the strings (the only such instance in both *Concertos*).

Bar 167 R.H. In **GE**piano the semiquaver beginning the bassoon motif was mistakenly granted the form of a grace-note. In **FE**piano (→**EE**) it was changed to a quaver. We do not take into consideration this correction, inconsistent with the rhythm of **A** and **M**orch (→**GE**orch), and possibly an on-the-spot correction of a mistaken record.

The solo part

p. 46
Bars 177-189 and 353-360 L.H. The slurs and dots accepted by us were introduced, most probably by Chopin, in the proofs of **GE** (→**FE**→**EE**). **A** does not contain dots, and the slurs are marked unclearly so that it is uncertain whether they are to encompass whole bars or only the second and third crotchet (they are absent in bars 354-356 and 358-360).

Bar 191 L.H. On the second beat **A** (→**GE**) has the *c¹-e♭¹-a♭¹* chord, which in the proofs of **FE** (→**EE**) Chopin altered to *a♭-c¹-a♭¹*.

p. 47
Bar 210 L.H. The main text comes from **FE** (→**EE**), where it could have been introduced by Chopin in the proofs. The variant is the **A** (→**GE**) version.

Bar 217 L.H. The sources of the solo part – **A** (→**Ge**piano →**FE**piano→**EE**) – have *F* in the bass. At the same time, the fundamental bass note in the orchestra part – **Re**F and **M**orch (→**GE**orch) – is indubitable *G*. At the beginning of the bar this gives an interval of the second as the foundation of harmony; it is difficult to accept that Chopin intended this in such an accompaniment. It is most likely that while writing **A** Chopin envisaged only the solo part (the orchestral parts in ½**A** were written by someone else), in which the real bass line in bars 213-218 is arranged as follows (smaller notes were used for writing the harmonic scheme of the higher voices):

Taking into consideration the whole sonority with the orchestra, the bass note in bar 217 must be *G*, since the lower sounds of the piano create, together with the cellos and double basses, the following progression:

There are no premises for believing that Chopin wished to change the fundamental bass note from *G* to *F* in this version. The necessity of solving the seventh would require altering the root also in the next bar (to *E♭*), which we do not find in any of the sources (such a change was introduced in some of the later collected editions).

Bar 219 R.H. The seventh quaver in **A** (→**GE**→**FE**1) is *g¹* (**A** shows that Chopin originally wrote another note, most probably *c²*). We give *b♭¹*, introduced by Chopin in **FE**2 (→**EE**).

Bars 220-221 L.H. **A** has the following version:

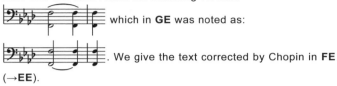 which in **GE** was noted as:

. We give the text corrected by Chopin in **FE** (→**EE**).

p. 48
Bar 237 R.H. ♮ before *f³* was added in the proofs of **FE** (→**EE**).

p. 49
Bar 243 L.H. The last chord in **FE** has a superfluous quaver flag, possibly owing to a misunderstanding during the proofreading (see below).

Bar 243-244 L.H. **A** contains the following version (in smaller typeface we give the cello and double bass parts according to the concurrent version unaltered by Chopin in **Re**F, **M**orch and **GE**orch):

In **GE** The solo part was changed as follows:

The final version, accepted by us, was introduced by Chopin in the proofs of **FE** (→**EE**). Some of the later collected editions arbitrarily compiled fragments of the **GE** and **FE** version.

Bar 248 L.H. In **A** (→**GE**) *f* on the first beat has the value of a dotted minim, and the *e♭♭¹-a♭¹* fourth – that of a minim. We give the rhythmic values amended by Chopin in **FE** (→**EE**).

Bar 252 L.H. On the second beat **FE** (→**EE**) mistakenly has the *c♭¹-a♭¹* sixth. We give the indisputable version from **A** (→**GE**).

Bar 253 In the sources the sign ***p*** is at the end of this bar. Chopin probably applied an old convention of placing the sign near the middle of its mandatory range (in this case: bars 253-254).

Bar 256 R.H. On the sixth and seventh quaver **FE**D has a pencilled annotation which could signify sustaining the sixth quaver:

We do not take these supplements into consideration since the deciphered version is uncertain, and its sound effect – taking into account the authentic pedal markings – imperceptible.

Bar 260 ½**A** (→**GE**→**FE**→**EE**) contains the following versions (the solo piano in Chopin's handwriting and the strings chord in another hand):

Attention is drawn to the mistaken record of the trill on ebb^3 (the absence of an accidental above this trill indicates f^3 as the top note, which is obvious nonsense). The inept voice-leading, in which the solo piano takes up the orchestra ebb^1 with a delay and only in the highest voice, also suggests an error. **ReF** makes it possible to identify this mistake: the part of the second violins should contain not ebb^1, but fb^1. Against the background of the authentic $gb\text{-}fb^1\text{-}bb^1$ chord the source version of the solo part could be recognised as corresponding to Chopin's intention; we give it in the main text.

The not completely parallel voice-leading – db^1 in L.H. passes directly to eb^1 in bar 261, while db^3 passes to eb^3 in the R.H. *via* ebb^3 – is a phenomenon encountered in several works by Chopin, such as *Concerto in E minor* Op. 11, second movement, bar 29 and third movement, bars 279-280, *Waltz in Gb* Op. 70 bar 56, *Fantaisie in F minor* Op. 49, bar 104 and 273 and possibly *Polonaise in C# minor* Op. 26 no. 1, bars 69-70. A similar situation occurred also in bars 243-244 of this movement of the *Concerto*, where Chopin ultimately smoothed out the harmonic progression (see commentary to those bars). Taking into consideration the above correction made by Chopin, and the fact that in the discussed place the alignment of db^1 and ebb^3, multiplied by means of a trill and not blended into the chord texture, appears more vividly, we propose the version given as a variant, in which a smooth harmonic sound is achieved at the cost of a slight modification of the rhythm (alleviated by the fermata).

Some of the later collected editions arbitrarily changed db^1 to d^1 in the triplet on the second beat, deforming the characteristic melodic motif in the L.H.

p. 51
Bar 285 and 287 **A** has *cresc.* in bar 285, prolonged with dashes to the end of bar 289. In **GE** (→**FE**→**EE**) this marking appears twice: in bar 285 and 287 (the strokes were overlooked). The repetition of the marking, unjustified here, probably testifies to Chopin's correction in **GE**. Two possibilities come to mind:
— Chopin shifted *cresc.* to bar 287, but the correction remained unfinished and the earlier printed marking was unnecessarily left (cf. commentary to bar 78 and 79);
— Chopin restored *cresc.* in bar 285, leaving the marking mistakenly printed in bar 287 as consistent with the preceding one.

Bar 296 L.H. The last note in **A** is mistakenly ab^1.

Both parts
p. 52
Bar 313 and 325 Only **M**orch (→**GE**orch→**FE**orch) contains the markings *ritenuto* in bar 313 and *a tempo* in bar 325.

The solo part
Bar 327 R.H. **FE** has mistakenly the grace-note ab^1.

Bar 329 L.H. There is no ♮ before the third third in **A** (→**GE**→**FE** →**EE**). An oversight by Chopin is proved by *a*, concurrently appearing in **ReF** and **M**orch (→**GE**orch). Cf. also bar 5.

Bars 330-331 L.H. Ties sustaining the $bb\text{-}db^1$ third were added by Chopin in the proofs of **FE** (→**EE**).

p. 53
Bar 337 L.H. In **GE** (→**FE**→**EE**) c^1 was overlooked on the first beat.

Bars 337-340 R.H. As a result of the overlapping errors made by Chopin and the engravers none of the sources contains the correct text:
— in **A** the line delineating the range of the *all'ottava* sign, which started on the second crotchet in bar 337, ends with the last quaver in bar 339; the word *loco*, used by Chopin to denote a return to the normal pitch, is also missing;
— **GE** added to the **A** notation a mistaken beginning of the 8va sign, which was shifted above the first crotchet in bar 337;
— in **FE** (→**EE**) the whole 8va sign was removed.

The discussed bars end the 16-bar period (bars 325-340), comprising particularly its melodic close. Their transference an octave higher than in analogous bars 1-16 deforms the course of the melodic line of the theme. Notation **A** is, therefore, unquestionably incorrect. This conclusion is confirmed by the later correction of **FE**, despite the fact that the proofreading was imprecise and unnecessarily eliminated the 8va sign above the second crotchet in bar 337 (the characteristic leap to the $f^3\text{-}f^4$ octave plays an important role in this part of the *Concerto* – cf. bar 13, 29-32 and 369-376).

Bar 340 L.H. In **GE** (→**FE**→**EE**) the note F at the beginning of the bar was mistakenly included into the solo part.

Reduction of the orchestra part

Bars 340-341 R.H. Instead of an accent on the third beat in bar 340 **GE** (→**FE**→**EE**) wrongly has a tie sustaining f^1.

Bar 344 R.H. **A** has rhythm ♩♪ on the third beat. In analogous bar 20 in **A** Chopin changed the rhythm to equal quavers. All the remaining sources have equal quavers in both bars.

Bar 345 R.H. In **FE** (→**EE**) the bottom note of the chord on the second beat is mistakenly g^1.

The solo part

Bar 352 R.H. **A** (→**GE**) does not have the note d^2 at the beginning of the bar. Chopin added it in the proofs of **FE** (→**EE**).

Bar 356 R.H. The penultimate note in **GE** (→**FE**1) is mistakenly g^2. Chopin restored bb^2 in the proofs of **FE**2 (→**EE**).

Bar 366 and 368 L.H. In these bars the sound of the last crotchets was shaped in three phases. **A** contains the following version:

In **GE** Chopin altered the bottom notes of the chords to B in bar 366 and c in bar 368:

In the proofs of **FE** (→**EE**) Chopin introduced the final version, harmonically the smoothest and the most convenient from the viewpoint of execution.

p. 54
Bar 369 L.H. Some of the later collected editions arbitrarily changed the highest chord note at the beginning of the bar to f^1.

Bar 388 R.H. The sources do not have an accidental before the bottom note of the third quaver, which should be read as eb^2. Some of the later collected editions added ♮ prior to that note. There are no sufficient bases, however, to regard the notation in the sources as incorrect (cf. the beginning of this progression with $c^3\text{-}eb^3\text{-}ab^3$).

Reduction of the orchestra part

Bar 392 R.H. The grace-note in **A** is the $c^2\text{-}ab^2$ sixth. The absence of the bottom note in **GE** (→**FE**→**EE**) could be considered as an oversight of the engraver or a correction made by Chopin.

p. 55
Bar 401 L.H. The first chord in **FE** (→**EE**) mistakenly has an additional note c^2.

Bar 404 R.H. **GE** (→**FE**→**EE**) overlooked d^2 in the second chord.

Bar 404 and 405 R.H. In the proofs of **FE** (→**EE**) Chopin added the note c^3 in the last chord in bar 404 and c^2 in bar 405. Similarly *ff* in bar 405.

The solo part

Bars 415-417 R.H. **A** does not have an *8ᵛᵃ* sign from the second beat in bar 415 to the first crotchet in bar 417.

Bar 415, 423, 455 and 463 L.H. On the penultimate quavers of the bars **A** (→**GE**) has $d\#^2$ (single or in a chord). In the proofs of **FE** (→**EE**) Chopin changed the script of those notes to eb^2.

Bar 416 **A** (→**GE**) has a crotchet $g\#^2$ (R.H.) and a quaver $g\#^1\text{-}b^1$ (L.H.). In the proofs of **FE** (→**EE**) Chopin altered them to ab^2 and $ab^1\text{-}b^1$.
L.H. In the three-note chord at the end of the bar **A** (→**GE**) has g^1 as the bottom note. In the proofs of **FE** (→**EE**) Chopin changed it to e^1.

Bar 422 L.H. On the third beat **A** has the $bb\text{-}f^1$ fifth. This is a remnant of an earlier version of the bar, with db in the bass (Chopin deleted this db on the first beat and wrote Bb). In **GE** (→**FE1**) Chopin changed the fifth to a third, but b before the bottom note was forgotten in an inaccurate correction. In the proofs of **FE2** the sign was mistakenly supplemented prior to f^1. **EE** has the correct text.

p. 56 *Bars 432-433* R.H. **GE** (→**FE**→**EE**) most probably overlooked the tie sustaining f^2.

Bar 433 and 437 R.H. The treatment of the quavers on the first beat of those bars as the first and third in a quaver triplet seems to be recommended both for musical reasons (the triplet motion rules indivisibly in the coda of this movement of the *Concerto*), and for the purposes of execution (transference of the hand). We encounter this type of notation in several of Chopin's compositions, e. g. in *Sonata in B minor* Op. 58, first movement, bar 54, first crotchet in the R.H. and fourth crotchet in the L.H. In the latter Chopin added in a pupil's copy a rest between two quavers (cf. *Performance Commentary* and *Source Commentary* about this bar).

Bar 435 It would be difficult to say whether Chopin wished to mark the pedalling in this bar. Initially, bars 435-436 in **A** had pedal markings (identical as in the following bars). Then Chopin deleted both signs in bar 436 and ❋ in 435. We do not know, therefore, if the mistake in the last bar consisted of deleting ❋ or leaving ℘.

p. 58 *Bar 476* R.H. Chopin wavered as regards the level of the last quaver. Deletions in **A** testify to two changes of decision: Chopin started with g^2, altered it to d^2, and then returned to g^2. **GE** has g^2, but in the proofs of **FE** (→**EE**) Chopin changed it once again to d^2. In the main text we give his last decision.

Bar 485 R.H. **GE** overlooked a^3 and a^2 on the first and fourth quaver of the bar. Chopin supplemented the missing notes in the proofs of **FE** (→**EE**).

Bar 486 R.H. The last quaver in **A** (→**GE**→**FE1**) is d^2. Chopin changed it to e^2 in the proofs of **FE2** (→**EE**).

p. 59 *Bars 489-490* Chopin carefully wrote the combination of the trill and tremolando (cf. first movement, bar 335) in notes, describing even the number of strokes (three groups with four strokes each). He erred, however, by marking their value as demisemiquavers instead of semiquavers. This mistake was revised in **GE** (→**FE** →**EE**), increasing the number of strokes to eight in each group, which is nonsense (it cannot be played in the tempo marked by Chopin, or even in one close to it).

Reduction of the orchestra part

Bars 491-492 The sources contain an indubitably flawed text, different in each source. The reason for the divergences and mistakes was probably the unclear notation in [**SI**] and Chopin's only partial participation in editing the orchestra part. Here are the source versions:

ReF

The bottom notes *C*, written in parentheses, are deleted with a pencil. Attention is drawn also to the distinctly mistaken second chord in the R.H.

Morch (→**GE**orch)

The sound of the fourth chord, which contains neither the note f, present in **ReF** and **FE2**piano, nor the sound bb occurring in **A** (→**GE**piano→**FE**piano→**EE**), gives rise to doubts. Emphasis should be also placed on the full four-note chord of the seventh in the last chord.

A

It should be stressed that the visible part of this fragment is not in Chopin's handwriting. Unquestionable errors include d^1 instead of c^1 in the fourth chord, and the absence of bb in the fifth one. **GE**piano (→**FE1**piano→**EE**) amended only the first of those mistakes, and omitted bb in the first chord.

FE2piano

Chopin introduced the change of e to f in the fourth chord during the last phase of the proofs (**EE** contains e).
Our conjecture takes into account the most certain elements of the sources – the first three chords according to **A**, the fourth chord in the version corrected by Chopin in **FE2**piano, and the fifth chord according to **M**orch (in an arrangement corresponding to the preceding chords in **A**). It is very likely that this version corresponds to Chopin's intention. As regards the most doubtful bar 492, the harmonic progression in the version accepted by us was used by Chopin – in a similar rhythm – in *Impromptu in F#* Op. 36, bar 31, 35 and analog.

Jan Ekier
Paweł Kamiński